Adjusting to An Older Work Force

Adjusting to An Older Work Force

Lois Farrer Copperman
and
Frederick D. Keast

VNR VAN NOSTRAND REINHOLD COMPANY
NEW YORK CINCINNATI TORONTO LONDON MELBOURNE

Copyright © 1983 by Van Nostrand Reinhold Company Inc.

Library of Congress Catalog Card Number: 82-21856
ISBN: 0-442-21493-6

Manufactured in the United States of America

Published by Van Nostrand Reinhold Company Inc.
135 West 50th Street, New York, N.Y. 10020

Van Nostrand Reinhold Publishing
1410 Birchmount Road
Scarborough, Ontario M1P 2E7, Canada

Van Nostrand Reinhold
480 Latrobe Street
Melbourne, Victoria 3000, Australia

Van Nostrand Reinhold Company Limited
Molly Millars Lane
Wokingham, Berkshire, England

15 14 13 12 11 10 9 8 7 6 5 4 3 2 1

Library of Congress Cataloging in Publication Data

Copperman, Lois Farrer.
    Adjusting to an older work force.

    Bibliography: p.
    Includes index.
    1. Aged—Employment—United States. 2. Aged—
Employment—Government policy—United States.
3. Retirement age—United States.   4. Retirement age—
Government policy—United States. 5. Employment
forecasting—United States. 6. Manpower policy—
United States.   I. Keast, Frederick D. II. Title.
HD6280.C64 1983   331.3'98'0973   82-21856
ISBN 0-442-21493-6

Preface

The purpose of this book is to provide a systematic assessment of policies implemented by both government and employers that influence the employment and retirement decisions of older workers. For several years the authors have directed various research projects exploring the effects of retirement-related legislation on employers' policies and workers' retirement behavior. Information obtained from employers, government personnel, and older workers has been gathered together in order to present a comprehensive picture of the many complex factors that affect the retirement decisions of older American workers. Numerous examples are provided to illustrate different employer-developed strategies that affect these decisions.

The basic premise of the book is that older employees base their employment and retirement decisions on the incentives and disincentives established by public and private policies. If government and/or employer policies provide penalties for continued employment or fail to reward full-time work, most older workers will tailor their employment decisions to their own maximum advantage and retire. The authors discuss the ways in which current policies encourage older individuals to retire and present extensive discussions of policy and program options that could result in marked changes in retirement patterns. Retirement patterns are sensitive to leisure and compensation preferences. If employers and/or government policy makers wish to influence the decisions of older workers, they must develop new alternatives that refashion the currently mutually exclusive states of retirement and work.

America's population is getting older. During the next two decades — as the number of younger workers entering the labor force continues its steady decline — the "baby boom" generation will be gradually approaching retirement age. The current debate over social security is a harbinger of the potentially destructive intergenerational battles that may occur in the twenty-first century if we do not begin now to deal with the impending joys and problems of an aging population.

This book was written to provide a systematic assessment of government and employer policies influencing retirement decisions and to offer models of policies and programs providing positive incentives to older individuals to remain in the work force. Throughout the book, the authors assume that, at best, government and employer policies should be "retirement neutral"–neither encouraging nor discouraging retirement. The aging of the population and the costs of social security programs may require that policies be adopted that encourage the continued labor force participation of productive and capable older individuals. There do not appear to be strong, sustainable arguments for continuing policies that usually encourage good and willing workers to retire.

Why should we be concerned with these issues now – twenty to thirty years before the real impact of the retiring baby boom generation? The primary reason is that today we have the ability to make decisions and experiment with both public and private policies before the sheer number of people affected by such policies is so large as to make mistakes extremely costly. Public policies must be changed now and phased in over time. Raising the retirement age or making other suggested policy changes cannot be easily or equitably done when the individuals affected are approaching retirement age. If policies are adopted now and phased in over a period of twenty years, the policies may be politically more acceptable, socially less disruptive, and economically more equitable.

The opportunity to experiment should be equally attractive to private employers. Currently, less than 20 percent of individuals aged 65 or older are delaying their retirement. Most workers are continuing to retire between the ages of 62 and 65 years. Employers who begin now to develop retirement policies that fit their companies in both a philosophic and economic way may experiment with different alternatives, see which work, and thereby establish effective personnel and remunerative plans that will not inconvenience large numbers of persons. As with people of all ages, older workers are not all the same. Management needs to develop policies that provide flexibility – encouraging older workers to stay whom they would like to see keep working and letting those they would like to retire go. If companies wait until problems in retirement policies are acute and the numbers of people involved are large, they will have missed a valuable opportunity. The solutions to the problems of the future will be much harder to achieve if both government and employers do not begin their preparations soon.

The authors had three primary audiences in mind while writing this book. The first was comprised of business executives, human resource planners, and other decision-makers. While constrained by a myriad of legislative and regulatory parameters, this group has proven to be an innovative force in the development of policies that serve the interests of both their firms and their workers. Time and time again, the authors have found that imaginative managers have developed innovative policies that have improved their companies' productivity by altering the retirement behavior of their older workers. Generally, these gains have been realized at no cost through the fine-tuning of existing personnel and remunerative policies. Yet, while firms with progressive policies of this type are by no means rare, no medium has existed through which successful experiments could be communicated to others interested in developing similar programs. The authors have received many inquiries requesting information about such programs and have provided it on an individual basis. We hope that this book will allow the employer audience to find out what other firms are doing as well as to obtain information on the incentives and disincentives to retire that exist in many existing personnel and compensation policies.

Administrators, legislators, and other government personnel comprise the second group that makes important decisions affecting older workers. Although their influence on retirement decisions is perhaps more indirect than that of employers — except perhaps in the area of social security — their decisions have a major impact on retirement patterns. Government regulations and legislation set the parameters within which employers may develop their own policies. In recent years, it has become increasingly clear that new directions in government policy are appropriate both for the benefit of the workers themselves and for the nation of which they are but a part.

The third audience to which this book is addressed is composed of academics, research staff members, and the many individuals who are concerned with "the greying of America." Although many are interested in older workers and would like to see them encouraged to contribute to the nation's productive capabilities, a lack of knowledge of employer policies and the ways in which employment and compensation decisions are made in the private sector hinders their ability to provide useful and specialized information to the employers who could benefit from it. We hope that the detailed discussions in this book will help bridge this gap so that pertinent gerontological information can be effectively incorporated in the policies of employers.

The help of many people and organizations has made this book possible. The background research and the findings reported throughout the book were funded through grants from the U.S. Department of Labor, the Administration on Aging, and the President's Commission on Pension Policy. The Institute on Aging, School of Urban Affairs, Portland State University provided the institutional support necessary for the completion of this work. Certain individuals have provided counsel, ideas, and comments. We would like to thank Elizabeth Meier and Malcolm Morrison, in particular, for their contributions. We also wish to express our appreciation to our colleague, Dr. Douglas Montgomery, who actively contributed to the research projects on which this book is based. Finally, we would like to thank our research assistants, Ms. Rita Field and Ms. Donna Stuteville. Their many contributions are gratefully acknowledged.

LOIS FARRER COPPERMAN
FREDERICK D. KEAST

Acknowledgments

The authors gratefully acknowledge the contributions of the personnel of the School of Urban Affairs, Portland State University, Portland, Oregon. In particular, the encouragement and substantive contributions of Dr. Douglas G. Montgomery have been most helpful. In addition, our gratitude is extended to Rita Fields. Portions of this work were supported by the Administration on Aging, U.S. Department of Labor and the President's Commission on Pension Policy.

Contents

Adjusting
to An Older
Work Force

1
Background Issues

In recent years retirement issues have emerged as the subject of heated debate and widespread interest. Media and popular attention have focused on the social security system — its role in maintaining adequate incomes among retirees and its present and future costs. Self-serving political posturing aside, most policy-makers currently agree that changes in the system need to occur, but consensus on the direction and scope of the changes has not been reached.

During the late 1960s and the early 1970s concern for the elderly poor resulted in significant increases in social security benefits and ultimately the linkage of benefits to changes in the Consumer Price Index (CPI). The high rate of economic growth during the 1960s and the large number of young "baby boom" workers entering the labor force obscured the eventual costs of these policies to the nation, and their impact on the labor market itself. Then as the economy slowed and social security taxes began rising, public attention shifted to the expense of continuing the present benefit levels and a reexamination of the social security funding mechanism which finances present benefits out of present wage taxes.

Retirement issues have occupied the national limelight to the extent that few people remain unfamiliar with the existence of the issues if not their root causes. Basically, the problem is one of numbers. Fluctuations in birth rates and medical advances between 1930 and the present have resulted in a present and future population which will be characterized by unprecedented growth in the older segment of the population at a time when the young working population will be shrinking. The age composition of the U.S. labor force will change dramatically during the next decades — the number of young workers will decline as the numbers of older individuals and retirees grow. Simple arithmetic suggests that the tax burden necessary to support present benefit levels under a "pay as you go" retirement system will consume an increasing percentage of the nation's income.

Although the retirement problem specifically related to social security funding is now well-known, serious consideration of the large-scale changes in the labor force's age composition which underlies the problems in financing social security has largely been neglected. Attention to short-term problems and an apparent myopia have impeded our ability to recognize and react to major labor force trends whose impact will go far beyond the problems in social security funding. During the past century, the American labor force has undergone four major periods of change as the U.S. has passed from an agricultural to an urban society. Labor market institutions of the next decades simply must be altered by the shifting composition and character of the changing workforce. The focus of this book is on changes in labor practices which affect and are affected by older workers. As this segment of the population grows in numbers and position, existing labor market institutions must eventually accommodate the changing environment.

There have long been reasons to suspect that retirement income programs have been luring able workers away from the job. Now and increasingly over the next 20 years, there are growing reasons to question whether we as a nation can afford to either lose their skills or support them in a comfortable retirement.

To an extent, these issues are well adapted to an economic interpretation. However, the abilities of individuals operating in any marketplace are constrained by limitations imposed by legal restraints and tradition. The market for labor – particularly the market for older labor – is constrained by a wide range of policies and practices. The actual impact and existence of many of the restraints on the market for older labor are, unfortunately, frequently unrecognized. Labor markets are complex institutions reflecting the mores and values of the culture, private and public income programs, personnel policies, technological developments, and a myriad of other factors. All of these factors work together to influence the labor market environment and the demand for and supply of workers.

In the long run, labor supply always equals labor demand: this axiomatic economic stipulation simply suggests that, over the long run, the intervening forces of time and price change will act to equalize the amount of labor available to the amount of labor employers chose to consume. Low prices for labor – wages – tend to drive people out of the labor force while high wages attract individuals into the labor force. Time is an important factor in this process: at any given point in time the levels of supply and demand may be unbalanced. Within limits, the adjustment processes which link the supply of workers with the demand for their services are very similar to those which operate in other market arenas.

Two important factors differentiate the market for labor from those for other commodities. First, and perhaps most important, is time. While various alternative mechanisms may speed the time necessary for the production of commodities, the "production" of new workers with the necessary prerequisites, such as secondary education, remains largely fixed at 18 years. Even if the demand for labor were to double tomorrow, new young labor force participants could not be produced to meet the new demand until the turn of the century. Thus, barring major immigration changes, the parameters of the labor market are known at any given point in time and labor market predictions have a high degree of reliability. The new entrants to the labor force of the next two decades are, by and large, already born. Deviations from labor market projections for the next 20 years are unlikely to be of sufficient magnitude to alter basic trends.

A second distinguishing characteristic of the labor market, and the primary cause of uncertainty, is the ability of potential participants to opt into or out of the market. This is a luxury which simply is not extended to other, inert factors of production. The large number of women entering the labor market in the 1970s and the steady decline in the labor force participation rates of older men illustrate the magnitude of labor market fluctuations caused by the availability of alternatives open to potential workers. Although there may be a sufficient number of people to fill available jobs, there is no assurance that they will do so. In general, fluctuations in the demand for and supply of labor may result in high levels of unemployment or alternatively in a shortage of workers.

During the past decade, the large number of "baby boom" workers and women entering the labor force combined with a general slowing of the economy, resulted in an abundance of labor supply and an apparent scarcity of job opportunities. The ready availability of labor, particularly young labor, resulted in the adoption of many private and public programs to encourage older individuals to leave the labor force. The short-term focus of the U.S. media, employers, and government policy makers has prevented a widespread realization that the period of labor abundance is ending and that new policies and practices are necessary for the future.

There are indications that current patterns of labor market behavior will lead to labor shortages during the next 20 years. Years of reliance on large numbers of new labor force entrants have produced employment and taxation policies which form the basis for today's labor market operations. These policies are based on the assumption of a large body of young workers which in the past has absorbed much of the impact of fluctuations in the economy. Since the 1930s, the emphasis in government policies and the practices of most private employers has been oriented toward younger groups in the labor force. The reverse side of this coin has been the creation of conditions which encouraged or required older workers to opt out of the labor force. In general, it is reasonable in light of historical records to suggest that the past 50 years of American labor history has witnessed a recurrent theme in which the removal — generally the self-removal — of older workers was seen as a mechanism to expand the opportunities of other labor force subgroups.

To say that older individuals themselves have been ill-served by this trend would be an oversimplification. By and large, recent surveys suggest that older Americans as a whole perceive retirement favorably. However, there is substantial reason to believe that many older individuals may have desired alternatives to full-time retirement that have not been widely available. Regardless, age has become a powerful criterion in determining labor force participation and in the valuation of labor by employers.

The practice of devaluation in accordance with most ascriptive criteria, such as age, race, and sex, is discriminatory and illegal under federal and many state laws. Age alone may not constitute a reason for a negative personnel action or discrimination in remuneration. Yet, institutional factors including personnel policies, tax policies and pension policies do vary in their effect with age. Employment and career practices have led to a general expectation, as well as the widespread reality, that older individuals — especially those over age 65 — no longer work. Instead they are supported by pension-based income streams, social security benefits and savings.

The disincentives in both private and public policies for older individuals to continue in employment are widespread. The following examples illustrate a number of the primary policies which encourage retirement. (These issues are discussed in more detail in following chapters.)

- Current retirement ages established by the Social Security Administration encourage retirement at age 65 with full benefits and age 62 with reduced benefits. The eligibility for social security benefits is a major factor in retirement decisions and the current retirement ages encourage capable and productive workers to withdraw from employment.
- The current social security retirement test discourages full-time work for most eligible beneficiaries by subtracting one dollar of untaxed, cost-of-living adjusted benefit for every two dollars of taxable earnings over a specified amount ($6,000 in 1982 for age 65 and over). The retirement test combined with the different tax treatment for the two income sources may well result in a 75% marginal tax rate on earnings over the threshold. This high marginal tax rate, continuing work-related expenses, and the value of foregone leisure provide strong disincentives for full-time work.
- The social security delayed retirement credit of 1% per year, which is awarded to workers who delay application for social security past age 65, acts as a further disincentive to delay retirement. Benefits foregone between ages 65 and 72 currently are not recouped through the receipt of higher benefits later, but are lost to the individual. An actuarially adjusted credit of approximately 9% a year would contribute to making the retirement decision "retirement neutral," e.g., it would neither encourage or discourage retirement.
- The Age Discrimination in Employment Act (ADEA) Amendments of 1978 do not require employers to continue pension benefit accruals in many pension plans past the normal retirement age — usually age 65. Although many employers have adopted pension policies which exceed the minimum standards, the legislation as written poses disincentives to work past the normal retirement age. Many employees who continue working

will receive the same pension benefits after their delayed retirement as they would have received had they retired earlier.

- Most private pensions require that an annuitant terminate employment with the employer prior to receiving pension benefits. An annuitant who returns to work for the same employer usually faces a temporary loss of pension benefits. This policy encourages older workers to retire from employment with the same employer in order to obtain pension benefits. If retirees wish to continue working and receive pension benefits, they generally must seek employment with a new employer. Due to real or perceived age discrimination in hiring, the retirees may become "discouraged workers" and withdraw completely from the labor force.
- Present personnel policies generally require full-time work. Although many capable older workers would prefer part-time work to full-time retirement, suitable part-time positions are not widely available.
- Present remuneration policies including fringe benefit programs are not specifically tailored to the needs or desires of many older workers. Available fringe benefit policies are usually aimed at satisfying the needs of a typical, young male, head of household.

The influences of these practices on the retirement and employment behavior of workers vary between individuals. Nonetheless, for all workers, as benefits associated with retirement rise — and particularly if some of these benefits are forfeited by continued work — the relative advantages of employment decline. As they do, people retire.

The practices and policies encouraging retirement are not new — they've been developing continuously since the first social security benefit check was mailed in 1940. What is new is the societal context within which the process continues to unfold. The U.S. society — particularly those components of the society which affect the labor force — is in a period of considerable change. The age composition of the population was discussed earlier. Another apparently changing factor which influences both work force composition and the ability of society to support a large nonproductive segment of the population is the slowing rate of economic growth.

This nation has been fortunate in recent years. Workers in the U.S. have been able to retire when reaching older ages. Their employment has not been necessary to their continued support and the economy has not vitally required their services in order to function. High rates of economic growth have permitted the luxury of expanding pensions − in essence paying people not to work. Economic growth also permitted the growth of policies which redistribute income from the young to the old. The relatively large national "cake" made it possible to promise generous programs to older individuals without a divisive political struggle. As the rate of economic growth has slowed, the size of federal programs and the cost of social security, in particular, have come under increasing scrutiny. Inevitable changes in the age structure of the adult population will exacerbate current problems even further in the future.

Retirement is not a "free" good or an automatic right. In many societies, including this one not so long ago, people worked until they died or were no longer able to work. The changes our society will undergo in the next few decades will hopefully not require that sick or disabled persons must work or forego income. The large majority of people will still continue to retire − but at later ages. In all probability full-time retirement at early ages will be the exception rather than the rule. Such changes in retirement patterns would relieve the pressures on the social security system and ensure that a large pool of capable workers would not be lost by productive enterprise.

As the debates over social security programs emphasize, it costs money to support people in retirement. Private retirement plans are − or, more accurately, will be once legally mandated full funding of pensions is attained in the year 2001 − fully funded. The contributions made to pension plans by employers are made at the time when the work is performed which qualifies the worker for a pension. If politically we can resist the temptation to utilize the tantalizingly vast pool of pension dollars for "socially useful" but imprudent investments, the fully funded pensions will be available as a reliable income source for retirees of the future.

Many public pension programs covering government employees are not currently funded. Providing the liberal benefits often promised through these plans may be a shock to future taxpayers. As mentioned previously, the social security program is currently financed so that benefits paid out at a given point in time are collected in taxes during that same time period. As the retirable population grows in the future and the younger population shrinks, it is reasonable to anticipate increases in the costs of the social security program for every individual and employer in the economy. In all likelihood, the size of the necessary increases will be dramatic and will precipitate socially divisive debates.

As the nation approaches the twenty first century, the rock and the hard place of retirement are well defined. Many older workers warmly embrace the concept of retirement and expect to be able to retire at relatively young ages. Through the years a complex set of incentives imbedded in retirement income programs, taxation policy, and employment practices have developed which tend to influence people into retirement even when they would prefer to continue working. At the same time, it is apparent that the already significant costs of these practices will increase dramatically in years to come. Moreover, older workers may well be needed by the economy as a whole and by individual employers within the economy.

In light of these quickly unfolding realities, there is reason to be concerned about the future. Two questions command attention: What needs to be done, and who should do it?

What needs to be done? In general, wide-reaching policies and practices which induce retirement should be identified and altered. Retirable workers are currently encouraged to opt out of the labor force. They can be encouraged to opt in.

In this respect, it is unrealistic to expect older workers to counter the forces which have influenced people into retirement and continue to work of their own volition. Events of recent years suggest that it is also unrealistic to expect the easy implementation of measures which would drastically alter the retirement benefits of those who are now retired or those who are close enough to retirement to have framed well-developed plans. There remains, however, a range of alternatives, many of which have been implemented already in various segments of the economy.

Who should do it? Two broad bodies of policy and practice affect workers: those generated by government and those of individual employers. Governmental policies affecting older workers include social security, taxation, and a range of legal restraints which govern the actions of employers.

Government programs and policies must fit the reality of the present and the future if they are to promote the "public good" rather than act as a drag on the society's productivity. A social security system developed during times of record unemployment and retirement ages which have little relevance to present mortality or health data must be modified to remain effective and viable. Nevertheless, the social security programs constitute a social contract. Their performance and predictability are important to the security of thousands of older individuals. Potential major modifications in the system must begin long before they are implemented to allow individuals to center retirement plans around new requirements. Future major alterations, such as raising the ages of eligibility, must be made now if they are to be politically viable.

Employers, in spite of legal parameters, retain a considerable degree of flexibility in the ways in which they affect workers' retirement decisions. Employment policies, work schedules, remunerative packages and retirement plans are among the influences determined by employers. Moreover, in spite of the decentralization of policy making functions among individual employers, there is considerable constancy in the policies of employers as they relate to older workers. Considering the expected changes in the labor market of the future and the high costs of continuing to encourage early retirement, employers must begin to reexamine their present policies. Just as older workers are a diverse group including many individuals with differing levels of skill and productivity, employers in the U.S. vary between corporate giants, such as IBM, to the "mom and pop" grocery store. In reading the following chapters, the reader should keep in mind that policies which have been advocated as benefiting older workers reflect differing costs and effects and are not appropriate to all employers. Various policies may be successfully adopted by some employers and not others. The internal structure of the firm, the composition of its labor force, the makeup of its production needs, the growth or decline of the firm and/or industry, the geographic location, and other factors contribute to its personnel requirements and the structuring of its remuneration policies. Firm size as well as its profitability and the structure or type of product or service generated are factors which must be considered in the adoption or rejection of various personnel and benefit policies. The importance of these and other factors in determining the best personnel and remuneration packages to fit the employers' and the employees' needs cannot be overemphasized. One particular personnel and benefit package will not fit the employment needs of diverse firms or older individuals.

Many employers are currently reviewing their older worker and retirement policies and developing and implementing new programs which will be described in further sections of this book. Many are seeking information on other employers' programs. But, employers need to carefully consider alternatives in light of their own current and future needs and adapt programs to suit their own particular requirements. Employers should obtain as much information as possible on the detrimental and beneficial effects of different alternative work patterns; specific information on labor force supply projections by occupation for their geographical area; methods for conducting an age analysis of their work force; retraining opportunities and experiences of similar employers, and the costs and benefits of alternative remuneration packages. In brief, employers must develop as much information as possible on different alternatives, and then develop and adopt the policies which are best suited to their needs.

In summary, then, both government and businesses are capable of influencing workers within their spheres of influence to alter retirement behavior. What's more, the results of policy changes in each setting can be materially affected by policies in the other.

This book explores these issues. Working from the premise that the retention of older workers in the labor force is in the interest of the reader — if not now, then later — the discussion begins with a broad treatment of shifts in the country's population which can be expected to affect the labor force over the next 20 years. Specific emphasis is placed on the roles of older workers now and in the future. From there, discussion turns to a detailed treatment of personnel practices and remunerative issues which can be employed to alter existing patterns in retirement behavior. Finally, the book concludes with a general discussion of the issues and recommendations.

2
Markets for Older Labor: The Next Twenty Years

INTRODUCTION

The labor market for older workers — if one can be said to exist — has proven in recent years to be a dynamic, complex amalgam of heterogeneous components. To speak broadly of a single market through which individuals barter their services involves prior assumptions of similarity both among the workers who comprise the market's supply and of the employers which generate demand. Neither conceptualization is accurate, and both generate simplistic views of complex phenomena.

Although it is often necessary, as in this discussion, to assess labor market phenomena on a broad scale, the very diversity and complexity of the processes through which labor is marketed makes it impossible to fully discuss the many influences and parameters involved. Predictions may be advanced, but the rapid pace of change in many of these markets is likely to make many such predictions out of date before their publication. Both factors impinge on the ability to predict with reasonable accuracy.

The development of policy nonetheless necessitates the generation of insights into likely future realities. Burkhauser's observation that many of social security's problems arise not out of disfunction but rather out of outdated concepts of social problems highlights this principle in reverse: if policy is to promote needed or desired conditions — if it is to permit rather than prohibit necessary change — it must be framed in the context of the future conditions it will affect and within which it must operate.[1]

It is the goal of this chapter to derive some sense of the future demand for and supply of older workers until the year 2000. More than the precise prediction of conditions, however, the discussion will emphasize the forces which are likely to influence the future, and will concentrate on identifying characteristics of labor markets within which change will most likely take place. Based on these discussions, attention will turn to labor issues which may become increasingly important as the next 20 years unfold.

The chapter includes four sections. The first section explicitly focuses on a brief analysis of likely changes in the U.S. population composition over the next two decades. Second, attention is turned to discussion of what constitutes a labor market. The third section addresses forces which may affect the demand and supply of older labor through the next 20 years. Finally, the chapter concludes with a broad discussion of how forces identified in the earlier sections can be expected to be reflected in the demand for and supply of older workers through the remainder of the twentieth century.

POPULATION

The short-range prediction of population composition constitutes a relatively safe endeavor — most citizens of the future are alive today. Since this particular discussion targets only 20 years into the near future and then focuses only on the population aged 20 years and above, the primary sources of error to be encountered involve mortality, immigration and unpredictable catastrophies. As with most other discussions of present and future populations,[2] this discussion draws on counts and estimates completed by the U.S. Bureau of the Census.

In assessing the distribution of the nation's population between various age classes, it is apparent that radical changes are underway. Table 2-1, which presents population projections by age class through the year 2000, illustrates these changes well.

The most striking shifts involve the declining numbers anticipated for the very young population — those between ages 0 and 19 — over the next 10 years: the 1980 total of 69.9 million individuals under the age of 18 represents the highest population in this age group expected prior to 1995. Even in the longer time frame ending in the year 2000, the growth rates anticipated among the very young represent less than half the rates of increase predicted for any other age group. Other elements of Table 2-1 derive significance from precisely this process. The babies born during the 1950s will continue to dominate the population pyramid as they age: through their sheer numbers

Table 2-1. Population projections (in millions).

	1980	1985	1990	1995	2000
0–19	69.9	68.1	69.4	71.3	72.2
20–24	69.9	68.1	69.4	71.3	72.2
25–29	18.7	20.1	19.5	16.8	15.4
30–54	65.2	71.8	80.6	88.2	90.8
55–64	21.1	21.6	20.5	20.2	22.7
65 +	24.9	27.2	29.7	31.2	31.5
Total	220.5	228.9	237.1	243.7	248.4
Median Age	30.3	31.7	33.0	34.5	36.0

Source: U.S. Bureau of the Census, *Current Population Reports,* Series P-25, No. 704, "Projections of the Total Population By Age and Sex for the United States: Selected Years, 1980 to 2050." Washington, D.C.: U.S. Government Printing Office, 1977, p. 86.

they produce rapid rates of growth in the age classes they enter, and distinct declines in the age classes they leave.

These patterns of growth and decline among different age classes are directly reflective of fertility patterns associated with different historical time periods. As reflected in Figure 2-1, completed fertility rates reached their peak during the late 1950s, approaching four births per female age 15 thru 44. From that point, however, fertility rates declined markedly and, excepting only one short period from 1968 to 1970, continued their drop through the late 1970s. In 1978, completed fertility rates were at their lowest point in 50 years and represented only about 1.7 births per female age 15 thru 44: this represents less than half the rate of only 21 years earlier and is well below the level associated with population replacement of 2.1 births per female.

Fertility rates are extremely important in issues relating to aging. Once established in an age cohort, subcomponents of a population largely retain their relative sizes with respect to other age cohorts. From the fertility rates shown in Figure 2-1, it would be reasonable to assume that members of the population during the 1930s would be less numerous than, for example, those born during any 10 year period between 1940 and 1970. Similarly, the low rates of reproduction generated during the 1970s produced an age cohort of smaller proportions than any other of the prior 50 years. Tempered only by age-specific catastrophic events (such as war) and immigration, the

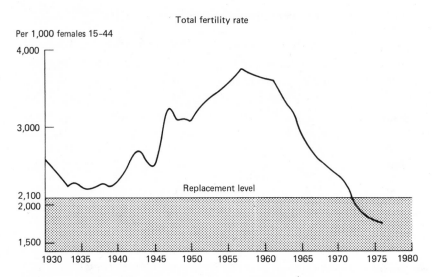

Figure 2-1. Comparison of total fertility rate with natural increase: 1930 to 1976.

Source: U.S. Bureau of the Census, "Estimates of the Population of the United States and Components of Change: 1940 to 1976, *"Current Population Reports."* Series P-25, No. 706, Washington, D.C.: U.S. Government Printing Office, 1977.

relative sizes of age-equivalent populations are frozen with respect to those which precede and follow. These relationships continue through time as the population ages.

Table 2-2 makes these processes more readily apparent. Table 2-2 reflects the proportion of the total population over age 19 in each of four age classes through the year 2000. Unlike Table 2-1, the group aged 0 to 19 years has been dropped from Table 2-2: consequently, figures represent the distribution of that portion of the population

Table 2-2. Population projections: percentage of population over 19 by age class.

AGE GROUP	1980	1985	1990	1995	2000
19–24	13.8	12.5	10.3	9.3	9.0
25–54	55.7	57.2	59.9	60.9	60.3
55–64	14.0	13.4	12.2	11.7	12.8
65 +	16.5	16.9	17.7	18.1	17.9

Source: U.S. Bureau of the Census, *Current Population Reports,* Series P-25, No. 704, "Projections of the Total Population By Age and Sex for the United States: Selected Years, 1980 to 2050," Washington, D.C.: U.S. Government Printing Office, 1977, p. 86.

which can realistically be expected to participate in the labor force during the next two decades.

Here again, it is apparent that the youngest class of individuals reflected in the Table is expected to decline considerably as a proportion of the population throughout the remainder of the century: the proportion of the labor force composed of new, young entrants has begun to decline and will continue to decline through the year 2000. The age range from 25 to 54, however, is anticipated to grow throughout the century, only beginning to decline in 1995. This growth reflects the movement of the baby boom cohort through the life span. Numbers of individuals age 55 to 64 will reflect little change until the year 2000, when again the aging baby boom will begin to enter a new age class. The older population will experience rapid growth throughout the century, reflecting the relatively high fertility rates preceding 1930.

In general, the population of the year 2000 will be older than that of 1980. A crude measure of population aging, the median age, will increase from less than 30 years in 1978 to over 35 years in 2000.

There is reason to anticipate that predictions relating to the future sizes of older populations may be conservative. Assumed mortality rates play a larger role in the prediction of more advanced age groups than among younger populations, and mortality rates are responsive to advances in medical technology. Rapid improvements in the treatments of illnesses which are leading causes of death have led in recent years to dramatic extensions of the life span, and have rendered conservative most past Census Bureau projections of older populations. This point is particularly well made by Sheppard and Rix (1977) in their observation that Census Bureau predictions of older populations have consistently proven to be smaller than the numbers actually counted when the time of predictions arrived.[3] In all, then, the growth in population predicted for the more advanced age classes is likely to be conservative. While it is difficult to incorporate into population predictions the effects of medical advances not yet made, the fact that earlier estimates have consistently fallen short can be taken as a warning in considering future predictions. If so, the aging trends identified above will tend to be more pronounced.

The labor force constitutes, for the most part, a sub-set of the population. Broad forces affecting the population can be expected to be reflected in the labor force as well. In the absence of other forces, it would be reasonable to anticipate that declining numbers of new workers from the youngest age groups will lead to escalations in demand for workers from the more advanced age classes, who will comprise unprecedented proportions of the national population. While this displacement of demand from young to old may well occur, it may be less than universal in scope and will likely be mitigated by the availability of labor from other subgroups. This subject constitutes the focus of the discussion to follow.

LABOR MARKETS

Many discussions of the role of older workers in the labor force tend to address both the supply and the demand for labor in terms of undifferentiated, homogeneous bodies of skills which, in their similarity, are largely interchangable. In a number of applications, this is appropriate. Members of given age cohorts, for example, are definitionally similar with respect to age. Similarly, firms experiencing rapid growth or sharp declines may also be broadly grouped. These similarities aside, however, it is reasonable to anticipate that units of analysis which are comparable with respect to some factors may well be quite different in other, important ways. A 62-year-old textile worker, for example, is not readily interchangable with a machinist of the same age. On the demand side of the market, hospitals experiencing an unfilled need for skilled nurses share little with oil extracting firms which cannot recruit drilling personnel or with oyster processers in need of shuckers. It is necessary to differentiate between distinct types of demand for labor and between dissimilar aggregates of supply. It is in this context that the concept of the labor market gains its relevance.

The term "labor market" has been defined as, "the geographical area within which a particular group of employers and wage earners buy and sell services."[4] Five general types of differentiating characteristics can be employed to distinguish between markets.

1. *Skill* constitutes a primary, perhaps even the most important, factor in differentiating between labor markets. As suggested above, the availability of an otherwise desirable textile worker is of little

benefit to the firm seeking a skilled machinist: the two are not sub-stitutable. Two differentiating characteristics apply. The first is the ability to transfer the skills of workers from one occupation to an-other; since the practices surrounding textile manufacture do not readily extend to those needed by machining operations, the two markets are distinctly different on this basis alone. Additionally, the degree of skill needed must be considered; while it may be possible to educate a novice machinist in a relatively short period of time, only years of training and experience can produce a skilled operator. Both constraints limit the degrees of labor mobility — the ability of workers to move from one line of work to another.

2. *Geographic scale and location* are also important in distinguish-ing between labor markets. While some markets can be appropriately conceptualized on a nation-wide or even world-wide scale, most are considerably smaller. The labor market for investment counselors, for example, is generally local in nature, while that for oil rig personnel is typically regional. By and large, the most significant determinant of scale and location in the identification of labor markets is the degree of concentration of the activity itself. The extent to which labor is mobile is constrained by two sorts of factors: those identified with the activity and the location within which it is carried out, and those associated with the workers themselves. High costs of living, for example, have been identified as a factor reducing labor in-migration to certain areas.[5] Age, on the other hand, has been iden-tified as a characteristic of certain classes of workers which seems to vary inversely with willingness to change residential location.[6]

3. *Industrial setting* is a third characteristic which distinguishes between labor markets. Where skills are common to a number of industries, inter-industrial mobility is likely to be a realistic compo-nent in the recruitment of labor. The availability of university engi-neering faculty, for example, to transfer their skills to private industry has been cited as a primary cause of current shortages of instructors in this field.

4. *Structure* is a fourth, less readily identifiable characteristic of labor markets. Phelps defines structure as, "a set of 'established prac-tices' which are applied consistently in carrying out the various em-ployment functions of recruitment, selection, assignment to jobs, wage payment, transfer, separation, and the like."[7] The use of union

halls in the assignment of individuals to jobs in certain fields constitutes one such structural characteristic, while seniority is a broadly recognized structural element of a different type.

5. *"Career track"* is a fifth distinguishing characteristic which has received little attention. Career track refers to the succession of positions and/or responsibilities which are realistically to be encountered in the career of a typical worker. Three such tracks would appear to predominate. In the first, the worker experiences little or no change in job responsibility throughout the career: most illustrative of this pattern, termed the "stationary career track," is the construction laborer, the farm worker, or the retail sales clerk. The second career track involves little change in activity, but identifiable differences in the degree of skill needed to satisfactorily complete successive responsibilities encountered during the worklife: machinists constitute such a group, and pursue a "horizontal career track." Finally, a third alternative involves the succession of the worker through positions of differing responsibilities: termed a "vertical career track," this type of career is common among administrative or managerial personnel in their attainment of escalating heirarchic positions within an organization. It is suggested that individuals in the first track are the most mobile of the three groups, while those in the second and third tracks reflect considerably less ability to change positions or type of work.

Together, these five characteristics tend to differentiate the functional, geographic, and processual components of labor markets. Each contributes uniquely to the promotion or limitation of workers' mobilities between job types, and each contributes uniquely to an inability to accurately portray labor issues in broad, undifferentiated terms. Succeeding discussion in this chapter will attempt to identify those components of the labor market which will most likely reflect change in the next two decades.

LABOR FORCE

The twentieth century has seen dramatic changes wrought in the forces which influence both the size of the population and its composition. In addition to the factors influencing the population from which it is derived, the labor force reflects changes which affect who enters, when they start, the means by which they withdraw, and the kinds of work they can aspire to attain. The place of the older worker in the labor force is similarly subject to significant change. The institutionalization of retirement, the parallel generation and expansion of retirement income sources, high inflation rates, a host of legislative developments, and dramatic drops in mortality all affect the association which links older workers to the labor force.

In this context, the discussion of the future with specific reference to older workers is at best risky. It is in part in recognition of these many uncertainties that this chapter undertakes a discussion of the topic rather than the presentation of predictions. More than this, however, the chapter avoids prediction precisely because the future is in part yet ours to shape. In that sense, what follows might be termed a scenario of future conditions based on the extension of present policies.

Older Workers Today

It is no secret that older workers are departing from the labor force in steadily increasing proportions. As reflected in Figure 2-2, the incidence of labor force participation among male workers over age 45 has declined with few exceptions throughout the last decade. These trends have continued since the late nineteenth century and are now well established.

While a number of factors have contributed to declines in the employment activity of individuals beyond age 45, the most important influence is widely acknowledged to be the ability to retire.[8] While 28% of those age 60 and 61 refrained from work in 1979, among those aged 62 to 64 eligible for social security benefits close to half chose not to participate in the labor force. Beyond age 65, only one in five workers continues in employment.

The role of retirement in declining labor force participation rates is presented in Figure 2-2. The proportion of newly entitled social security beneficiaries who were less than age 65 in 1978 was 70%, up from 55% in 1962. While a greater proportion of women than of men submitted applications for early retirement in 1978, members of both sexes are retiring earlier than they did in previous years.

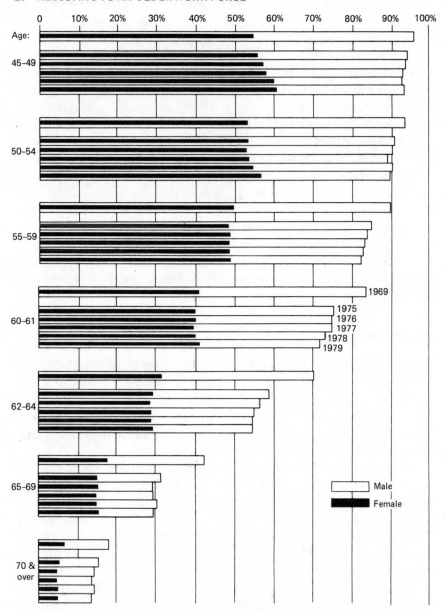

Figure 2-2. Civilian labor force participation rates for persons aged 45 and over, by age and sex, 1969 to 1979.

Source: Bureau of Labor Statistics. Employment and Earnings, various January issues and unpublished data.
Source: Shirley H. Rhine. *America's Aging Population: Issues Facing Business and Society.* The Conference Board, Report No. 785, 1980.

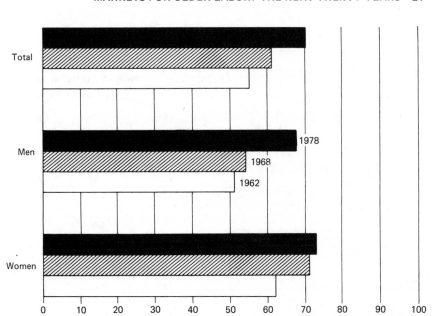

Figure 2-3. **Proportion of newly entitled beneficiaries aged 62–64 years, 1962, 1968, 1978*.**

*Men became eligible for actuarially reduced social security retired worker benefits at ages 62 through 64 in August, 1961: women had become eligible in 1956.

Source: Social Security Administration. Social Security Bulletin, September, 1979.

Source: Shirley H. Rhine. *America's Aging Population: Issues Facing Business and Society.* The Conference Board, Report Number 785, 1980.

These trends notwithstanding, over half of the men and almost three out of ten women remain involved in the labor force through age 65. They are, however, concentrated in certain occupations. Table 2-3 dramatizes this point. Older workers tend to be overrepresented among farm workers, managers and administrators, and service workers. While many of the entries in Table 2-3 reflect lessening concentrations, it is also apparent that among farm personnel, the services, and a limited range of professional classifications the high concentration of older workers is relatively stable or expanding.

At the risk of oversimplifying, three factors seem to promote this pattern of differential distribution.

Table 2-3. Occupations with high concentration Index[a] for selected male age groups, 1970 and 1977.

OCCUPATIONAL GROUP	CONCENTRATION INDEX MALES 55-64 YEARS		
	1970	1977	CHANGE
Engineers	95	133	+28
Physicians, dentists and related practitioners	126	116	-10
Managers and administrators, salaried, manufacturing	143	155	+12
Managers and administrators in other industries	130	122	- 4
Managers and administrators, self-employed in retail trade	160	174	+14
Managers and administrators, self-employed, other	157	170	+13
Carpenters	126	105	-24
Foremen, nec	143	153	+10
Machinists and job setters	135	114	-21
Metal craftsmen, excluding mechanics, machinists and job setters	134	132	- 2
Farmers and farm managers	149	145	- 4

OCCUPATIONAL GROUP	MALES, 65 YEARS AND OVER		
	1970	1977	CHANGE
Physicians et al.	200	208	+ 8
Health workers, except practitioners	152	18	-134
Other professionals, self-employed	354	249	-105
Managers and administrators, self-employed in retail trade	189	177	-12
Managers and administrators, self-employed, other	194	208	+14
Sales workers, retail trade	135	121	-14
Bookkeepers	240	226	-14
Carpenters	159	115	-44
Cleaning service workers	243	185	-58
Personal service workers, except private household	146	182	+36
Protective service workers	170	161	- 9
Farmers and farm managers	426	515	+89
Farm laborers and supervisors	170	164	- 6

[a]The concentration index is constructed by dividing the percentage of a particular age group in a particular occupation by the percentage of the total number of workers in that age group. If 20% of all male workers are aged 45-64 and 40% of mineworkers are aged 45-64, then the concentration index for mineworkers aged 45-64 is 200 (40/20 X 100). When the concentration index is 125 or over, we term it "high."

- Older workers are heavily concentrated among positions which demand experience and/or demonstrated ability. Thus, older workers are highly in evidence among physicians, managers and administrators, and foremen.
- Older workers are heavily concentrated among positions which offer flexibility in work involvement. This premise is supported by the high incidences of older workers among the self-employed and various of the professions. Older workers may prefer part-time to full-time work.
- Older workers are heavily concentrated in declining industries. New entrants to the labor force tend to gravitate in industries which are experiencing growth and offer favorable employment conditions. However, as these industries stabilize their allure to new cohorts of younger workers wanes and the age structure of the industry advances.

The role of older workers in the labor force 20 years from now will reflect a range of influences which are unique to the older workers themselves, and to other components of the labor force. The pages to follow address selected factors seen as most likely to shape the quantitative and qualitative characteristics of that role.

Older Workers: The Next Twenty Years

The demographic trends identified earlier with respect to the country's population will directly affect labor force composition. Other things being equal, alterations in the structure of the population from which the labor force is derived must ultimately be reflected in the labor force itself. "Other things being equal" constitutes a significant qualification, however. The composition of the labor force, like the population, changes. The central measure through which changes are reflected is the labor force participation rate, that proportion of a given group which is engaged in or seeks paid employment. As reflected in Figure 2-4, labor force involvement among selected groups has fluctuated considerably over the past 25 years.

If present trends continue, the Department of Labor (DOL) expects the role of older workers in the labor force to decline even further. Meier and Ditmar report DOL projections of labor force

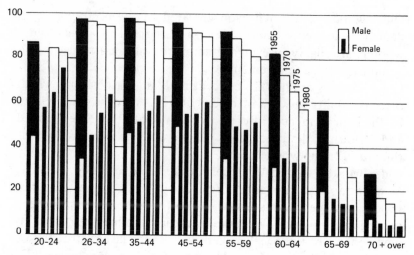

Figure 2-4. Participation rates of the civilian labor force by age and sex, 1955, 1970, 1975, and 1990.

Note: 16-to-19 year olds not included.

Source: Bureau of Labor Statistics. Howard N. Fullerton, Jr. and Paul O. Flaim. "New Labor Force Projections to 1990." *Monthly Labor Review,"* December 1976 and unpublished data (1976).

Source: Shirley H. Rhine. *Older Workers and Retirement.* The Conference Board, Report Number 738, 1978.

participation rates among older workers under each of three assumptions which differentially treat the strength of recent trends.[9] As reflected in Table 2-4, even the most liberal of these assumptions suggests diminished participation rates among all advanced age classes through 1995. However, the reader should bear in mind that these projections are based on assumptions which essentially project current conditions into the future. One important determinant of the future labor force — recent shifts in fertility rates — is thus included. Other factors, however, are more difficult to predict. Of great importance to the potential supply and demand of older labor are the potential effects of continued inflation, changes in social security legislation, and the shifting roles of other labor force subgroups.

Table 2-4. Projected total labor force participation rates of persons 55 and over, by age and sex, according to 3 different assumptions.[1]

SERIES AND AGE GROUP	MALES						FEMALES					
	1979	1980	1985	1990	1995	2000	1979	1980	1985	1990	1995	2000
A. High												
55 and over	47.3	47.2	46.1	43.5	42.2	43.7	22.8	22.7	22.1	20.7	20.2	21.2
55 to 59	83.1	83.2	83.3	83.5	83.7	83.9	48.5	48.7	49.8	50.8	51.5	51.8
60 to 64	62.9	62.9	62.9	62.8	62.7	62.7	32.9	32.9	32.9	32.9	33.0	32.9
65 to 69	29.4	29.4	29.4	26.6	24.6	23.8	14.5	14.5	14.5	13.6	13.0	12.8
70 to 74	19.1	19.2	19.1	18.1	17.3	17.0	7.5	7.5	7.5	6.9	6.4	6.3
75 and over	9.3	9.3	9.3	8.6	8.1	7.9	2.7	2.6	2.6	2.4	2.3	2.2
B. Medium												
55 and over	46.2	45.5	41.9	38.0	36.0	37.1	22.5	22.3	21.0	19.0	18.7	19.6
55 to 59	82.1	81.7	79.5	77.6	76.3	75.8	48.3	48.4	49.0	49.5	49.9	50.1
60 to 64	61.1	60.1	55.7	52.0	49.4	48.2	32.4	32.2	31.1	30.1	29.4	29.2
65 to 69	28.0	27.3	24.0	21.2	19.2	18.4	14.0	13.8	12.8	11.9	11.3	11.1
70 to 74	18.6	18.4	17.1	16.0	15.2	14.9	7.1	7.0	6.3	5.7	5.2	5.1
75 and over	9.0	8.8	8.0	7.3	6.8	6.6	2.5	2.5	2.3	2.1	2.0	1.9
C. Low												
55 and over	45.1	43.9	37.5	32.2	29.7	30.5	22.1	21.7	19.5	17.2	16.2	16.9
55 to 59	81.3	80.4	76.1	72.5	69.9	68.9	47.6	47.5	46.6	45.9	45.4	45.2
60 to 64	59.9	58.4	51.2	45.2	40.9	39.1	32.0	31.5	29.2	27.3	26.0	25.4
65 to 69	25.9	24.2	15.9	13.1	13.0	13.0	13.6	13.2	11.1	9.3	8.1	7.6
70 to 74	17.7	17.0	13.7	10.9	8.9	8.1	7.0	6.7	5.6	4.6	4.1	3.8
75 and over	8.4	8.0	5.9	4.1	2.9	2.4	2.4	2.3	1.8	1.4	1.4	1.4

[1] (A) High series assumes constant 1977 annual average rates for each age-sex-race subgroup of the population. (B) Medium series assumes constant rates to 1980, then a drop at one-half the trend rate for 1970–77. (C) Low series assumes continuation of the 1970–77 trend, unabated.

Source: U.S. Department of Labor, Bureau of Labor Statistics, November, 1978. In Meier and Ditmar, 1980.

Inflation and Labor Force Participation Among Older Workers

A central factor affecting the labor force involvement over the next 20 years will be the level of inflation in the economy, and the availability of alternatives to full-time work. Chapters 3 and 4 address alternative work and pay options, but inflation merits explicit discussion here. Under currently prevailing circumstances, most individuals seem to prefer retirement to work.[10]

However, pre-retirement decisions and satisfaction with retirement are each associated with financial well-being.[11] Because of its deleterious impacts on the real value of fixed cash flows and assets, there is good reason to anticipate that current and anticipated high rates of inflation will tend to lead workers to delay their retirements, or return to work as means of augmenting pension and asset positions, and as a means of lessening the period during which inflation can affect their standard of living.[12] While it is apparent that this effect has not yet led to reversals in long-standing trends toward early retirement, it is not clear that this resistance to inflation will continue indefinitely. As reflected in Table 2-5, a recent survey involving workers covered by TIAA-CREF found that a substantial majority had established retirement plans based in part on the potential impacts of inflation. These responses led researchers to conclude that, "inflation had affected the retirement planning of more than three-quarters of respondents," and that, "in looking ahead to retirement, the respondents were most concerned about their financial circumstances and the future course of inflation."[13] Should high rates of inflation continue,

Table 2-5. Extent to which inflation has affected retirement plans.
(Base = 1,438 TIAA-CREF participants.)

EXTENT OF IMPACT	PERCENT
A great deal	40
Some	32
A little	9
None	11
Not certain	5
No answer	3

Source: James M. Mulanaphy. "Plans and Expectations for Retirement of TIAA-CREF Participants," Washington, D.C.: Gerontological Society, November 24, 1980.

and should they continue to become more of a factor in the long-term planning of those contemplating retirement — as well as those who have already retired — it is reasonable to anticipate higher rates of labor force participation among retirable workers.

Continued inflation may generate two types of impacts on the labor force.

- First, reduced retirement rates would tend to force individual employers to adopt new approaches in their personnel plans. Existing promotional policies and practices would require adjustment in response to the lessened availability of vacancies opened by retirement, and sound means of dissociating unproductive older workers from the firm would be increasingly necessary.
- Second, to the extent that retirement rates decline, it is reasonable to anticipate heightened pressures for employment and remunerative packages which are more consistent with the needs and lifestyles of people in the advanced age brackets.

Interaction Between Older Workers and Other Labor Force Components

Up to this point the discussion has concentrated primarily on issues which would affect the supply of older workers. While issues of supply and demand in any market are closely associated, the demand for older workers will be in large part determined by the supply of other types of workers, and the types of positions they are able to fill. Accordingly, the discussion to follow addresses likely trends in the availability of labor among other age classes and among females over the two decades to come.

Young Workers. There is no question but that young workers — particularly males — will decline as a proportion of the labor force through most of the remainder of the century. As was noted in earlier discussion, the group aged 20 to 24 will decline in gross size through 1995. Additionally, male labor force participation rates are projected to decline slightly throughout this period. In light of these factors it is reasonable to anticipate that diminishing supplies of younger, male workers will lead to some degree of enhanced demand for employment of other groups in the labor force.

Middle-aged workers will increasingly dominate the labor force throughout the next two decades. The expansion of this age group as a component in the population is a direct result of the aging of the "baby boom" cohort. Female members of this age group are expected to have higher labor force participation rates than in the past. The expansion of participation rates among women in this group is likely to enhance even more the importance of this cohort in the labor force.

For middle-aged workers the principal job-related issues of the next two decades involve access to higher levels of responsibility and earnings. The pyramidal shape of the promotional hierarchy dictates that at each higher level of responsibility there are fewer spaces available. Due to the large size of the middle-aged population during the next two decades, promotional opportunities may become successively longer. Because promotional opportunities within a firm are created by growth and turnover as well as by retirements, the direct effect of altered retirement plans — should they become evident — on the youngest group of workers is likely to be negligible.[14] Potential conflict is more likely to arise between retirable workers and middle-aged workers aspiring to their positions. Firm-specific bottlenecks may generate increased transfers among companies. Labor mobility among middle-aged workers may escalate.

Female Labor Force Participation Rates

The labor force participation rates of women have been growing constantly and rapidly among the younger age groups since 1955. In the group including those aged 20 to 24 years, for example, participation rates have expanded from less than 50% in 1955 to about 65% in 1975, with further growth to over 75% predicted for 1990. Generally participation rates decline with age due to changes in both the extent and duration in employment.[15] Women workers tend to fall into two groups: those who work regularly and those who do so only occasionally. Female workers were approximately evenly divided between full-time and part-time work in 1974.[16] The employment pattern of this group is apparently directly associated with education, prior labor force participation, number of marriages, and the number of children. Based upon trends and observations evident in 1976, as many as 75% of women age 45 thru 60 will be in the labor force shortly after the turn of the century — up considerably from current levels.

Predicted levels of female labor force participation rates are based largely on future fertility rates — a measure which can change dramatically in a short period of time. Female labor force participation has expanded dramatically among those ages 20 to 44 in a period of constantly decreasing fertility. Experience suggests that fertility and employment are linked recursively, not only through direct associations but also by a range of other factors including fertility and employment plans, age at marriage, income and a host of others.[17] Especially in the short run, fertility has a large impact on a woman's employment. The effects of children on employment diminish in intensity as children approach school age. In brief, it would appear that fertility affects female labor force participation primarily through its interruption of worklife and less as a permanent prohibition to work. Nevertheless, interruptions lead to eventual re-entry into the labor force in positions of lesser responsibility and pay than would have occurred if employment had been continuous.

The female labor force is not universally distributed throughout industries or job types. Despite dramatic increases in the incidence of women among such prestigious and demanding careers as managers and physicians, DOL figures still reflect tremendous and growing overrepresentations of women among typical female jobs such as secretaries, bank tellers, and cashiers. In short, although the female labor force participation rates are likely to increase in the future, their jobs are not likely to be uniformly distributed throughout the economy.

CONCLUSION

The discussion of the preceding pages may be synopsized into a few brief statements:

- The labor force participation rates of older workers have fallen steadily throughout this century. The trend toward early retirement has accelerated in the past two decades.
- Those older workers who remain in the labor force are disproportionately concentrated in certain classes of employment.

In particular, older workers are likely to be engaged in part-time employment.

- Middle-aged workers — between ages 25 and 54 — will comprise an ever-expanding proportion of the labor force in the next two decades. The bulging middle-aged cohort is likely to exert increased pressure for the early retirement of older workers to increase their own promotional opportunities.
- Female workers in all age groups will increase their labor force participation throughout the next 20 years. The preference for part-time work among many women workers is likely to continue.
- The number of younger workers entering the labor force will decrease sharply during the next two decades.

The labor force changes discussed above are likely to bring a number of changes for older workers. Older workers in full-time work will face the largest population of middle-aged labor ever experienced in this country. Although these middle-aged individuals are likely to experience more constrained opportunities than preceding age cohorts, they have dominated the employment policy of the last decades and are likely to bring about changes in future policies. A strong, persistent demand for early retirement and other policies to increase promotional opportunities for this group are likely to occur in the next 20 years. Older workers in stationary career tracks are likely to experience relatively constant or increasing demand as competition from younger workers declines. Older workers involved in part-time work are likely to compete with women pursuing discontinuous career tracks. Opportunities for part-time work will expand as the two primary sources of labor — older workers and women — increase their demand for part-time positions.

To the extent that older workers are concentrated in slow-growth industries and companies, competition with younger workers will be diminished. The actual level of demand for these workers will vary with rates of industrial decline, and with the degree to which jobs in the industry are available in other industries. Demand for older workers in geographic areas of slow growth or decline will likely remain constant or growing, subject to the health of industries already concentrated there. To the extent that these areas also reflect high costs of living which impose barriers to in-migration, demand for older workers will be higher.

In sum, it is reasonable to suggest that the labor market for older workers in the future will be highly fractionalized, with determinants of supply and demand being largely unique to each individual market setting. In lieu of major alterations in relevant policy, however, it would appear that demand will not be the primary force establishing the parameters of those markets. Supply, reflecting expanding access to retirement, will likely continue to be the most important factor in shaping the labor market for older workers.

FOOTNOTES

1. Richard Burkhauser. Written testimony to the Subcommittee on Oversight of the Committee on Ways and Means, U.S. House of Representatives, *Hearings on Work, Retirement and Social Security,* September 10, 1980.
2. Jerome M. Rosow and Robert Zager. *The Future of Older Workers in America.* Scarsdale, New York: Work in America Institute 1980. Also, Elizabeth L. Meier and Cynthia Ditmar. *Varieties of Retirement Ages.* Washington, D.C.: President's Commission on Pension Policy, November 1979.
3. Harold L. Sheppard and Sarah E. Rix. *The Greying of Working America.* New York: Free Press, 1977.
4. Gordon F. Bloom and Herbert R. Northrup. *Economics of Labor Relations.* Homewood, Illinois: Richard D. Irwin, Inc., 1965.
5. Lois F. Copperman and Fred D. Keast. *In the Wake of the ADEA Amendments.* Portland: Portland State University, 1980.
6. Shirley H. Rhine. *Older Workers and Retirement.* New York: The Conference Board, 1978.
7. Orme W. Phelps. "A Structural Model of the U.S. Labor Market," *Industrial and Labor Relations Review,* April 1957.
8. Burkhauser, op. cit.
9. Meier and Ditmar, op. cit.
10. Herbert S. Parnes et al. *From the Middle to the Later Years.* Center for Human Resource Research, Ohio State University, 1979.
11. Ibid.
12. Copperman and Keast, op. cit.
13. James M. Mulanphy. "Plans and Expectations for Retirement of TIAA — CREF Participants," paper prepared for the Gerontological Society, Washington, D.C. 1980.
14. Stephen R. Cantrell and Robert L. Clark. "Retirement Policy and Promotional Prospects," unpublished paper, North Carolina State University, Raleigh, N.C. (Undated).

3
Personnel Policies

INTRODUCTION

Personnel policies which define the structure and hours of employment, standards for promotion, and employment benefits influence the job-related decisions of all categories of workers. Although personnel policies may treat all workers in the same manner, different labor force subgroups may, in fact, have differing levels of skills and experience in addition to different employment preferences. In theory the labor force may be composed of substitutable "units"; in reality employee skills and preferences may vary by age, sex, and other factors.

The preponderance of personnel policies currently in force among most U.S. employers are based on the assumption of a homogeneous workforce — primarily consisting of adult male heads of households, working full time and dependent on their wage and salary from one employer for their income.[1] These policies have persisted despite the fact that adult male full-time workers comprise less than 40% of the labor force. Although such policies may have been suitable for the labor market of the past, policies tailored to the needs of the young male breadwinner fail to provide the flexibility needed to accommodate a changing workforce consisting of two-earner families, women working full and part-time, and older workers eligible for or receiving retirement benefits related to previous employment.

Current policies were generally developed during a period of labor supply surplus. The abundant labor force supply of new job seekers as well as women returning to the labor force allowed employers to suit employment practices to their own needs. The labor market of the 1970s with the ready available supply of new entrants did not require employers to alter policies in order to successfully compete for workers. In the 1980s, the demographic trends which underlie labor force statistics will force many employers to review past personnel practices. During the next two decades labor shortages will oblige employers to search for new sources of labor supply as well as accelerating the substitution of capital for labor. A careful examination of population statistics suggests that the prime source of supplementary labor supply — able and qualified individuals not in the labor force — will be older individuals.

Even if employers have a strong preference for young workers, the numbers of individuals in this age group is dropping sharply. Burger King, a fast food chain which has relied on a teenage labor force, has already recognized the reality of demographic changes and has begun recruiting workers over 55.[2] Likewise, the potential pool of unemployed women will not be available as a major source of new labor in the 1980s. Although the percentage of women working may continue to rise slightly, the majority of women interested in and available to work are in all likelihood already working. The bulge of the population in the prime labor force ages are also employed and will not serve as a source of supplementary labor. Consequently, the most readily manipulable potential pool of workers will consist of persons in the older age groups.

The labor force participation rate for persons age 55 years or more has fallen dramatically during the past two decades. In 1979 only 62% of men aged 60 to 64 were in the labor force compared to 75% in 1970 and 78% in 1960. If present trends and policies encouraging labor force withdrawal continue throughout the 1980s, the Bureau of Labor Statistics estimates that by 1990, 30% of persons aged 55 and over will have withdrawn from the labor force. Although a proportion of the older individuals retiring from the labor force do so because of poor health, a substantial number withdraw because of their inability to find work or the existing policies which provide incentives for retirement. During the 1980s the population of older individuals mentally and physically capable of performing productive activities will include several million potential workers. Labor supply constraints of the next decade will require the development of new personnel and government policies which will "persuade" these individuals to engage in labor force activities. With the youth labor pool shrinking employers will develop new incentives and premiums to retain, retrain and reemploy older workers.

Research on older employees indicates that there are presently many ways in which employer personnel policies fail to meet their benefit and employment preferences. For the most part, workers age 50 and over have raised their children and purchased their homes, cars, and other major consumer items. Increasingly, older individuals are also part of dual earner households. Policies which provide coverages for dependents and other benefits for persons in their earlier years are not motivating rewards for this age group. Policies which limit opportunities for advancement with age, reduce opportunities for retraining and fail to reward experience operate as disincentives for older individuals. Most of these workers have devoted 30 or more years of their lives to full-time work. Flexibility in working hours which provide opportunities for developing and scheduling leisure activities have a strong appeal to this age group. Remunerative policies which allow older individuals to allocate benefit dollars to retirement related benefits rather than current earnings may also be preferred. Changes in personnel policies which reflect these preferences may be important to employers wishing to retain existing workers or employ new older workers.

This chapter and the following chapter will discuss a number of alternative personnel policies which are of particular relevance to older workers. The remainder of this chapter will be devoted to a discussion of various personnel policies and programs which affect older workers. The discussion will include an overview of the incidence of part-time work, a presentation of its pros and cons, and a discussion of the appeal of part-time work to older workers.

PART-TIME WORK

Part-time work which may be either permanent or temporary, allows employees to work less than the prevailing standard number of hours each week. Due to varying definitions of part-time work, the data on the number of employees working part-time is inexact. The U.S. Bureau of Labor Statistics defines part-time employment as less than 35 hours per week, but does not provide information on permanent versus temporary part-time jobs. Regardless of the exact definition, part-time employment of all kinds has increased rapidly in the U.S. in the past 25 years as seen in Figure 3-1. Part-time employment which is regular and voluntary included 14% of the labor force in 1979. In 1978 approximately 14 million persons in the civilian labor

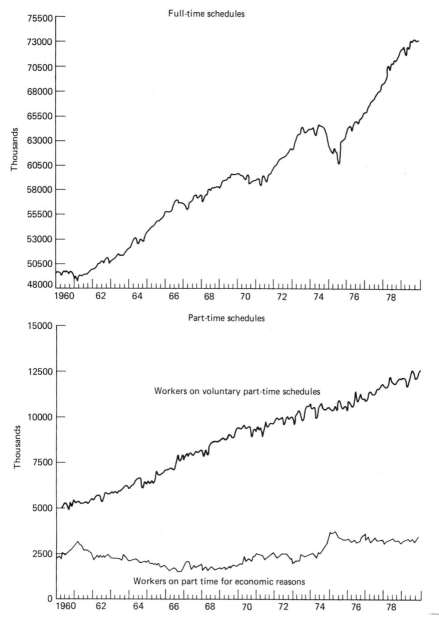

Figure 3-1. Persons at work full and part time in nonagricultural industries. (Seasonally adjusted)

Source: Bureau of Labor Statistics, 1977.

force were voluntarily employed in part-time work. Although part-time jobs have grown in absolute numbers, the percentage of voluntary part-time employees in the civilian labor force has not increased since 1972. Only 2.1% of all part-time workers are working part-time because they couldn't obtain full-time employment.[4]

Generally part-time workers are either young or old — nearly half of all workers who are under 20 or over 65 are part-time. As seen in Figure 2-2, the percentage of employed persons over 45 years of age who worked part-time rose sharply between 1969 and 1979 — especially for persons 65 years and over.[5] Nearly half (49%) of all those age 65 plus in the labor force are working part-time. The rate of part-time employment among the 65 plus group has increased despite decreases in the overall employment rate of this group. The increase in part-time work among older persons of both sexes probably reflects the greater availability of part-time jobs in recent years, as well as the increased interest in part-time work among this group.[6]

A recent survey by the authors of private firms nationwide found that part-time work options were the most commonly provided alternative work option — 22% of the responding firms had implemented or begun to implement part-time options. An additional 12% of the firms were seriously considering adopting part-time options. Only 50% of the employers were *not* considering adopting such policies.[7] Although a large number of firms use permanent part-time employees (Nollen estimates in the range of 55 to 75%), typically only 2 to 7% of their employees are part-time.[8]

The distribution of part-time jobs is highly related to industry and occupation. By far the majority of part-time jobs are located in the retail trade and service industries. Part-time work is least common in managerial and blue collar jobs and in the manufacturing industry. While managerial jobs could theoretically be adapted to part-time, in many firms norms about managerial availability and lengthy hours make it unlikely that large numbers of managerial jobs will be available on a part-time basis.[9] Similarly, organized labor's opposition to increasing the availability of part-time work is likely to limit the growth of part-time options in skilled occupations.

Part-time jobs have been developed by employers for a variety of reasons. The five reasons cited most frequently in previous studies for the development of part-time jobs are:

1. General or specific labor shortage.
2. Peak load coverage.
3. Extended hours of operation.
4. Job does not require full-time attention.
5. Retaining experienced workers no longer able to work full-time.[10]

During the next two decades labor shortages and the need to develop attractive options to retain or attract older workers are likely to become increasingly important reasons for the development of part-time jobs.

The Pros and Cons of Part-Time Work

Previous studies have indicated that some jobs are more suited to part-time employment than others. Jobs requiring continuous process technology or those requiring continuity, such as management positions, are more difficult to adapt to part-time employment due to scheduling and supervisory problems. Jobs thought especially suited to part-time work include those with discrete and/or repetitive tasks as well as stressful positions. Jobs with cyclical demand or extended hours of operation are also thought to be well suited to part-time employment. Regardless of its suitability, permanent part-time employment generally has not been institutionalized as a regular employment option.[11]

In a careful study of 68 firms, including both firms which utilized part-time work and those who did not, Nollen found that there are *no* compelling reasons why most job and work technologies are particularly suited or unsuited to part-time employment. However, continuous process operations and supervisory responsibilities are two work technologies that do appear to constrain the use of part-time employment. Other work technologies thought to be unsuited to part-time work, such as jobs requiring teamwork, problem solving, or extensive communication were not found to be constrained by part-time employment.[12] On balance the Nollen study and others have found that the economic benefits of part-time employment outweigh the economic costs.

About half the organizations that utilize permanent part-time employment report that the job performance of their part-time workers is better than their full-time counterparts.[13] Productivity is often improved due to less fatigue and the ability of a worker to keep up a faster pace for a shorter time — especially in repetitive jobs or those which are emotionally or intellectually taxing. Productivity may also rise because the part-time workers themselves are better than the full-time workers. In one-third to one-half of the cases studied absenteeism, tardiness, and turn-over records of part-time workers were actually better than those of full-time employees.[14] Turnover may also be reduced because of the increased time available to employees to manage personal problems or because job frustrations may be lower when a person does not confront them on a full-time basis.[15]

From an employer's perspective, the most frequently cited problems with part-time employment are supervision, administration, the loss of fringe benefits, and union opposition. Because workers are not available at all hours, supervisors may have increased problems in coverage and scheduling. In the past, part-time employees have generally not received the same fringe benefits as full-time employees. While most do receive paid vacations and holidays, only half receive sick leave. Less than half have generally received group health and life insurance benefits.[16] The cost of providing fringe benefits may be greater for part-time workers than full-time. In many cases, benefits such as vacation and pensions can be prorated to hours worked or salary and thus not cost proportionately more. In the case of workers age 65 and over the cost of providing health insurance may actually decrease due to the presence of Medicare. The employer cost for pension benefits may also be reduced if pension benefit accruals are not continued for existing employees past age 65 or if pension benefits are not provided for new hires who are within 5 years of the normal retirement age.

Despite the problems mentioned above, available research indicates that almost any job can successfully be scheduled on a part-time basis. There are no absolute technological barriers or major costs to part-time employment. For many the resistance to widespread part-time employment options would appear to be based on tradition and resistance to change as well as the common assumption that part-time workers are immature, unskilled, or lacking in their attachment to the labor force.

The findings reported in the preceding section were based on studies of employers who employed all types of part-time employees, not just mature, older workers. The conclusion that most jobs could be adapted to part-time employment would appear to be especially true when an employer is recruiting from the group of experienced older workers, including current employees interested in reducing work hours.

Part-time employment options for older individuals are receiving increasing attention in the U.S. Generally, experience and skill limitations have restricted the labor supply of part-time workers available for positions requiring high levels of skill, training or experience. But, these attributes are not lacking in the older labor force, a labor force subgroup with growing interest in part-time employment. The economic advantages which accrue to employers of part-time workers in general may be increased further when part-time employees are drawn from older workers.[17]

In fact, many of the objections to part-time employees disappear when the employer recruits part-time help from older workers with established work histories. For instance, a study by William Werther found that most supervisors generally conceive of part-time workers as young and unskilled. Consequently, they do not seek part-time help due to concerns about worker dependability, turnover, absenteeism and tardiness. Older workers do not lack job skills and have a low incidence of job turnover and absenteeism.[18] When older workers are solicited from the employer's existing labor force or retirees they also offer the additional advantage of firm and/or job specific experience and training.

A number of advantages which may result from providing part-time work to older persons are listed below:

- *Skills:* The skill level of older workers generally matches those of the labor market as a whole. Most older workers have many years of job experience and have a proven history of labor market involvement. Work habits are well developed.
- *Turnover:* Older workers have lower turnover rates than younger workers. Older individuals are less mobile and less likely to job-hop than younger workers. Older persons are generally settled and stable and have fewer personal demands placed on them by dependent family members.[19]

- *Motivation:* During many years of employment, older workers have developed self-discipline and a mature approach to job responsibilities. They tend to be conscientious, reliable employees.[20]
- *Job Security:* Due to perceptions of age discrimination or other factors, older workers frequently believe that obtaining new employment is difficult. This perception may result in increased importance of existing employment.
- *Productivity:* Currently available evidence indicates that there is little or no difference in the ability of older workers to perform on the job compared to the ability of younger workers. There is greater variability in learning ability within the group of older workers and within the group of younger workers than between younger and older workers — in other words, older workers must be evaluated individually just as younger workers. Years of experience and previous knowledge of work processes may allow older individuals to compensate for inadequacies. Experience and good work habits may also reduce the need for supervision or training.

Part-time older workers may offer the employer an available, reliable, experienced labor force with many of the same abilities — and problems — as full-time personnel. Although the number of older individuals working part-time is increasing, additional information on the costs and benefits of employing this labor force subgroup is needed. As presented in the following discussion, the interest in part-time employment among older workers is likely to grow during the coming decades.

The Preference for Part-Time Employment Among Older Workers

During the past decade a number of surveys and studies have found that full-time retirement may not be the optimal choice for many older persons. During the same period in which labor force participation rates for older workers has been steadily declining, a number of attitudinal surveys have found that many older persons would like to maintain their labor force attachment. A Harris survey in 1974 found that 30% of the respondents over 65 (over 4 million people in the general population) would like jobs. More persons in lower income ranges desired jobs than those with higher incomes.[21] A 1978 Harris poll found that while only 13% of the retired respondents were working on full or part-time jobs, more than half indicated they would have preferred to continue working instead of retiring — 23% would have preferred to work part-time as long as possible. Among current employees 24%* of all workers surveyed indicated a preference for part-time work rather than retirement, with about half saying they would prefer to work either full or part-time.[22]

Harris polls which measure attitudes cannot be assumed to accurately predict behavior. Nevertheless, such polls indicate a preference for flexible employment options rather than full-time retirement among a significant number of current workers and retirees. Surveys of both older workers in the general population as well as in-house employer surveys have supported the finding that most older workers who wish to continue working past the retirement age would prefer to work part-time or at a less demanding job.

Herbert Parnes in examining 1976 data on retired men from the National Longitudinal Study (NLS) found that only about one in every five retirees was in the labor force (only one in twenty worked on a full-year basis, while 10% worked at least half a year). Of those retirees who were employed, part-time jobs were more common. Almost three fifths worked under 1,000 hours during the year preceding the interview. The vast majority of the men working after retirement were receiving considerably lower hourly earnings than their preretirement job. The median real average hourly earnings declined by 39% for white males and 32% for black males.[23]

Several recent research studies provide new information on the subject of part-time work among older workers. Although limited in their scope, each of the studies investigated the issues of reduced hours among workers and retirees in more detail than has been available in previous works. The following discussion provides data on

---

*Interestingly, 46% of the self-employed preferred part-time work to retirement. The higher percentage may reflect these workers' abilities to realistically work part-time as opposed to other workers for whom part-time work may not appear to be as viable an alternative.

the alternative work preferences of older workers and/or retirees, the types of workers likely to desire part-time work, and other factors.

A study by S. Anschell of non-academic staff at the University of Washington (U. of W.) over age 55 and retirees of the last 5 years explored the potential for the phasing down of work involvement through reduction in hours or workloads. The study's findings indicate more workers may currently be considering changing to part-time jobs prior to full retirement than was true in the past. Although only one in five retirees reported considering working part-time as a step toward retirement, over one third of the pre-retirees were considering part-time work. The longer a person had been retired the less likely they were to have considered part-time work as a step toward full-time retirement. The increased visibility and acceptance of part-time work as a viable alternative may explain the changing attitudes.[24]

The University of Washington study also found that those considering part-time arrangements have a number of distinguishing characteristics. The older individuals interested in part-time work:

- "tend to hold relatively high level jobs which they perceive as important to meeting their needs;
- expect to miss work more than their counterparts;
- believe the change to part-time would both prolong their work life and improve their health;
- are not heavily involved in outside activities and see a reduced schedule as an opportunity to develop outside interests;
- have given a great deal of thought to when to retire; and
- have accrued relatively little retirement service credit."[25]

Interest in part-time work is not limited to persons in low level unskilled jobs or persons who have a weak attachment to the labor force. Part-time work is viewed as a way to maintain work involvement among persons who view work activities as a valuable part of their lives.

McConnell, Fleisher, Usher, and Kaplan had similar findings in their study of the desirability of work options among older workers at Lockheed Corporation, a large private aerospace corporation, and the City of Los Angeles. The study examined the feasibility of work options from the employer, union, and professional association perspectives. "Briefly, the major findings of the study indicate that most of the older workers responding planned to retire early (age 62 to 65) or very early (age 50 to 61). But although planning on early retirement, most individuals expected to have inadequate retirement incomes — three out of four expected to receive retirement incomes of one-half or less of their working wage. Not surprisingly, nearly half of the respondents planned to work after retirement. If alternative job options were available in their present jobs, one half of the respondents stated they would continue working past their planned retirement age for their current employer. The most popular job option selected by the older worker was part-time employment. But, particularly for Lockheed workers, part-time options were of interest only if they could draw at least part of their pension. Most respondents also indicated a preference for continuing on their current job rather than transferring to less demanding jobs — job modifications or transfers were undesirable if they required a reduction in pay."[26]

As in the University of Washington study, certain characteristics were found to be associated with a preference for part-time work. Part-time work was preferred by:

- College-educated workers.
- Those with positive attitudes toward retirement.
- Professionals.
- Those in high stress jobs.
- Those with 30 years or more of service with the same employer.

Full-time jobs were preferred by:

- Non-college educated workers.
- Those with negative attitudes toward retirement.
- Unskilled workers.
- Those in low stress jobs.
- Those with fewer years of service (1 to 15 years) with the same employers.[27]

In short, the study found that older workers desiring work options for continued work past their expected retirement age were generally in good health, involved in their work, and obtained personal satisfaction from their employment. Their decision to continue working is at least in part related to financial necessity. Thus the study findings suggest that older workers interested in work options are likely to be the same workers who employers would prefer to keep on the job. To retain them in their current jobs, employers must recognize the financial incentives which encourage these workers to terminate their present employment. The older workers are interested in reduced hours, — but if they are unable to receive at least part of their pensions, most of these individuals would opt for retirement from their present job with full pension. Nearly half would then seek a job with a different employer.[28]

Managers interviewed in the study were generally surprised at the significant amount of interest in work options expressed by their older workers. Similarly union representatives were unaware of worker interests and opposed part-time jobs to protect full-time jobs and to protect jobs for younger workers.[29]

In Spring 1981 the authors conducted a survey of workers age 50 and over employed in a large western high technology company. They also found a strong interest in part-time work among respondents.[30] In general, the older individuals responding to the survey appeared to be healthy, productive employees who were satisfied with their current job. Respondents included production workers, craft workers, managers, professionals, clerical workers, technicians and service personnel. The median age of the respondents was 57, the average length of service with the company was 13 years, and 53% of the participants were women. Approximately two-thirds of the older workers expressed an interest in part-time work as a step between full-time work and retirement. The most common reasons for interest in part-time work were the desire for increased leisure and more time for family activities.

The appeal of part-time employment as a transitional step between full-time work and retirement varies significantly by the type of worker, the worker's income, the length of service with the firm, and the worker's age. Managers, craft workers, and professionals expressed the most interest in part-time work while production workers, and service workers expressed the least interest.

The strong interest in part-time work expressed by managers may be of particular interest. When asked to describe how their job might be hypothetically modified, the majority of managers indicated they would prefer a job with fewer daily responsibilities. Four out of five would like jobs which would allow them to have more assignments which utilize their particular expertise.

Surprisingly, a higher percentage of men — 67% — were interested in part-time schedules than were women — 57%. The median earnings of workers expressing an interest in part-time work were $15,000 to $20,000 compared to the $10,000 to $15,000 gross earnings of workers not interested in part-time employment. As reported in the preceding studies, the higher income workers in this study are also more interested in part-time work than are the lower income workers.

The most prevalent part-time schedules currently available in the U.S. are part day, full week and full day, part week schedules. Few permanent part-time jobs are available on a part year basis. Almost one half the individuals in this study who were interested in part-time work indicated a preference for full-day, part week schedules for the full year. Approximately 40% of the workers were interested in a part year, part-time job.

Interest in part-time work is significantly related to the individual's perception that part-time work is an available alternative. Although a large percentage of workers surveyed were interested in part-time work as a transitional step to full time retirement, the number might have increased further if all workers had been aware that part-time work was available. 50% of the workers who did not think that part-time work was an available alternative indicated that they were *not* interested in part-time work compared to 30% of the workers who perceived part-time work as a possibility.[31]

The University of Washington study reached similar conclusions. Among preretirees at the University of Washington who believed the part-time option was available, 14.5% reported interest in taking advantage of it. Only 5.6% of those who did *not* think the part-time option was available were interested in part-time work.[32]

These findings suggest that employers who clearly promote the availability of a permanent part-time options may increase the numbers of workers expressing an interest in part-time employment. The clear availability of such an option is likely to result in potential retirees giving more consideration to part-time work as a realistic alternative to full-time retirement.

The findings of these studies which explore alternative work options for older workers in greater depth than they have previously been reported are generally consistent with one another. Each discovered considerable interest in part-time work among older workers as a preferred alternative to full-time retirement. Each study found that although older workers were aware of the potential costs of accepting part-time employment with the same employer, many would prefer to exercise this option if possible. Finally, all of the studies indicated that those expressing interest in part-time options possess characteristics which make them desirable employees.

Employers wishing to retain existing workers by offering permanent part-time jobs will need to carefully coordinate their part-time policies with their remuneration policies. The creation of permanent part-time jobs which do not penalize employees in terms of pension benefits is more likely to result in the retention of older employees.

Respondents in the three preceding studies clearly communicated their joint consideration of the benefits of part-time work and its impact on present or eventual pension benefits. University of Washington respondents reported that pension calculations would be an important factor in their decision concerning part-time work. The current defined benefit pension formula is based on the final average salary of the highest 2 years. A reduction in work hours and consequently salary would penalize persons to the extent that they would miss cost of living or step increases which would have raised their final salary. Respondents appeared to be quite aware that in periods of double digit inflation, cost of living increases and other raises may be important in calculating their pension benefit − e.g. 10% raises over their last 3 years would have a significant effect on pension benefits. If electing part-time work alternatives resulted in pension reductions, respondents were likely to continue working full-time.[33]

Presently, most private pension policies require that an employee cease employment with the pensioning firm before they may receive pension benefits. Generally, if the firm policy permits, employees may work less than 20 hours per week while receiving pension benefits, but past this point the workers' pension benefits are reduced or terminated. If an older worker is unable to receive pension benefits while switching to a part-time schedule, the employee may be motivated to cease work entirely or to seek work with another employer in order to begin receiving pension benefits. The older workers at Lockheed are clearly aware of the limitations of their firm's pension policies. Among workers interested in part-time work, 93% indicated they would not consider part-time employment if they did not receive any of their pension benefits. If they could not receive all or part of their pension while shifting to part-time work for the firm, most persons interested in part-time work would simply retire completely and seek a job with another employer. The present policy which does not allow shifting to part-time employment while receiving pension benefits, provides an important incentive for workers to switch employers in order to receive full pension while continuing in employment. The older individuals surveyed are not interested in substituting wages from work for pension benefits if they cannot increase subsequent retirement income.[34]

Finally, analysis of the data on over 900 workers over age 50 in a high technology company provides interesting insights into the relationship between interest in part-time work and remuneration. As in the Lockheed study, older workers expressed a strong interest in receiving pension benefits after shifting to part-time work. Three out of four workers supported changing pension policy to allow pension beneficiaries to return to work part-time for the same employer while receiving pro-rated pension benefits. Sixty-two percent of the individuals indicated that if they could receive pro-rated pension benefits for part-time work, they would probably or definitely continue to work part-time for their present employer past the age at which they currently expect to retire. The ability to receive pension income while continuing in part-time employment would provide a strong incentive for continued work and would enable the company to retain the services of many employees who would retire completely from the company under present policies. Management concerns that the availability of two sources of income to some employees would have a negative effect of the morale of other workers appear to be unfounded. Over half of the workers indicated that policies which allow pension as well as employment income would serve as an incentive with a positive effect on worker's morale. Almost two out of every five workers indicate such a policy would have no effect on their morale and only 8% indicate the policy would have a negative effect on their morale.[35]

Companies interested in gaining flexibility in their workforce may find that part-time alternatives for older workers aid them in solving personnel problems. The strong interest expressed by older workers in part-time employment may allow employers considerable flexibility in developing policies which fit the organization's employment needs while fulfilling the desires of older workers. Presently a number of companies perceive expensive early retirement bonuses — whether in cash payments or through the provision of normal retirement age benefits to early retirees — as their primary tool for manipulating the composition of their older workforce, and particularly their managers. Such policies are frequently costly not only in dollar terms, but in the loss of experienced employees who are familiar with the organization's policies. Data from the authors' study of older workers in a high technology firm indicate that many of the individuals who would be interested in a company offer to permit retirement at 55 with full unreduced benefits are also interested in part-time work with their present employer. Nearly one-half of the individuals sampled expressed probable or definite interest in such a policy. Managers were more interested in both early retirement bonus policies — 62% — and part-time work schedules — 77% — than were other types of workers. The strong interest in part-time work among managers in this and other studies suggests that organizations which learn to utilize part-time managers may be able to affect their promotional pyramids, retain the experience of older managers and reduce pension bonuses.[36]

Summary

In the years ahead as the number of new young entrants to the labor force continues its steady decline, employers may find that offering permanent part-time jobs enables them to attract or retain talented workers who are not available for full-time employment. Even if the national unemployment rate is high, there are often shortages in particular job categories or in certain geographical areas. The creation of part-time jobs may aid an employer in tapping "new" supplies of labor. This is especially true in the case of older workers who, faced with the choice of full-time work or retirement, have increasingly chosen to retire. The availability of permanent part-time jobs would attract persons who wish to reduce their working hours but who for economic, psychological, or social reasons would like to retain their attachment to the labor force on a part-time basis. The labor pool of experienced, mature older individuals either approaching retirement or already retired is currently a largely untapped resource.

In providing part time options to present full-time employees, employers should consider the effect of the transition on the worker's pension benefits. If the option of part-time work will result in lowering future pension benefits, workers are unlikely to elect this option. The benefit payout structures of an employer's pension plan may need to be modified so that the election of part-time employment during the last years of employment does not reduce future pension benefits.

Employers interested in attracting or retaining older workers should also design their programs around the institutional constraints which currently provide disincentives for older persons to work. In the case of part-time work — the most attractive alternative work option to most older persons — employers must consider the earnings ceiling of the social security "retirement test" and pension plan rules which prohibit many employers from paying out pension benefits to their own employees. The latter is a policy which employers may wish to re-evaluate and alter if they wish to retain their older employees.

In the past, most part-time jobs have been concentrated at the lower rungs of the career ladder, in service and clerical jobs and in retail and service industries. Only recently have part-time jobs been increasing at higher levels of pay and responsibility. For part-time jobs to be attractive to older workers as an alternative to full-time retirement — particularly for males — more high level jobs in a wider range of industries and occupations will need to be developed. Research studies indicate considerable interest in part-time employment among older workers who are college educated, professionals, administrators, and managers. Providing jobs for higher level workers may require employers to initiate job redesign, job sharing, and/or the negotiation of voluntary demotions. Once again, employers developing such policies must consider the effect on pension benefits and other remuneration policies if they desire to develop a successful program.

When developing fringe benefit packages, employers interested in developing jobs which attract or retain older workers should take into consideration the different preferences of older workers for fringe benefits. Workers who have already raised their families may have different priorities for fringe benefits than younger workers.

The development of personnel policies which permit flexibility in the hours of work and options in the election of fringe benefits will enable organizations to better utilize experienced older workers. Available research and experience indicates that such policies will have strong appeal to older workers and would encourage the continued labor force participation of older workers.

FLEXITIME

Flexible working hours, alternatively termed flexitime or flextime, offer employees the opportunity to choose their own arrival and departure times within limits set by management. A central element of flexitime programs is the "band width," which establishes the hours within which work must be completed. The band is usually 12 through 16 hours a day, rather than the standard eight hours. Employees must meet work time requirements within this period. The time band — which is almost universally established by the employer — is divided into core time and flexitime. Core time is a period during which everyone has to be on the job. The flexitime represents the hours within which employees can decide for themselves when to work.[37] Common core times are 10 A.M. to noon and 3:30 P.M., but the core may be varied to meet the needs of the working unit. Employees often may accumulate credit hours or debit hours — hours worked which are more or less than the number required during a reporting period.[38]

Flexitime allows workers to choose their own hours of work within certain constraints. In doing so, it provides the workers with the ability to determine their own schedules — shifting control to the worker and, to some extent, away from management. Flexible scheduling allows employees to schedule dentist appointments, classes, and other activities during the work week while still meeting their employment responsibilities. Flexitime advocates, including many employers who have adopted the system, state that the system increases employee morale and job satisfaction, reduces turnover, and eases problems of absenteeism and tardiness.[39] Employees, for example, are less likely to take a sick day to go to the doctor or exhibit chronic tardiness due to child-care problems. Employees may accomplish these activities during their free time gained by working earlier or later than normally allowed.

A number of studies report that flexitime results in productivity increases. Such gains are attributed to the fact that flexitime makes organizations work better.[40] In recent surveys "the median proportion of companies and employees using flexitime that subjectively reported increased productivity was 45%. The median size of productivity gains according to actual measurements of output per worker was 12% with most gains running from 5 to 15%." The measurements covered a variety of settings and industries.[41] Because the freedom allowed under flexitime is an attractive benefit, flexitime scheduling may also aid in recruiting new employees.

The success rate for flexitime is high − in two studies, 92 to 97% of employers adopting the program have continued to use the system. Flexitime appears to have few serious disadvantages and is easier to implement than other alternative work options such as the compressed work week.[42]

In a 1979 nationwide survey of private firms, the authors found that approximately 17% of the organizations had or were beginning to implement flexitime programs.[43] In 1977 approximately 2.5 to 3.5 million workers, or 6% of the labor force, were on flexitime. Flexitime is utilized in all industries, but is more common in finance and insurance firms and less common in manufacturing.[44]

The attractiveness of flexitime to older workers and its importance as an incentive to delay retirement are largely unknown. A recent study of older workers in the City of Los Angeles and Lockheed found that flexitime with full-time work was the second most attractive work option for older workers. This option was chosen by 11% of the workers (same job, flexitime full-time) as their first choice among options presented. Interest was greater among Lockheed workers than those at the City of Los Angeles.[45] In a study of older workers in a high technology firm, the authors also found that flexitime hours appeal to older workers. Although part-time work was the most popular work option selected, one in four of the respondents indicated that flexible hours would lead them to consider delaying their retirement by 1 year if they could keep their present job responsibilities.[46] If employers wish to retain their workers on full-time schedules, they should consider offering flexible work hours as an additional attraction. The opportunity to schedule more leisure activities may be particularly attractive to individuals approaching retirement. Although flexitime may allow increased work hour variability, it is unlikely that its availability alone would be a major factor in the retirement decision.

THE COMPRESSED WORKWEEK

A compressed workweek is the scheduling of the "standard" 40 hour/ 8 hour per day workweek into alternative segments. The common pattern is to compress the 40 hour week into 4, 10 hour days — the 4/40. Less typical are compressed schedules which comprise 3 12 hour days or 7 consecutive 10 hour days with the following week off — the 7/40. Usually the scheduling of the workweek is arranged to provide a 3 day weekend with employees working Tuesday through Friday or Monday through Thursday.[47]

Scheduling of different employees' work arrangements allows the employer to cover many different hours of operation. Variations in the days or hours when work is required can be scheduled to fit demand.[48] Employers that must be open round-the-clock or continuous process manufacturers may develop complex compressed workweek schedules and work-hour variations to meet their needs. For example, pharmaceutical firms which employ continuous process technologies may utilize work cycles alternating between 3 day and 4 day weeks respectively, including day and night shifts as well as weekends. Some hospitals have adopted the 7/70 to provide continuous nursing coverage and other employers have elected to utilize compressed schedules to provide maximum utilization of expensive computers.[49] The compressed workweek is generally more attractive to employees if scheduling results in 2 or more consecutive days off.

The compressed workweek is generally adopted to increase employee morale, reduce absenteeism, tardiness and turnover, and hopefully increase productivity. Many organizations utilizing the compressed workweek have estimated that productivity has either increased or at least remained the same. One of the primary societal and individual advantages of the compressed workweek is the reduction in rush hour traffic congestion. Employees working 10 hour days usually schedule their arrival and departure before and after rush hours. For workers this results in savings in the cost and time of travel. The compressed workweek received considerable attention in the early 1970s. From 1970 to 1973 the rate of adoption of the program was constantly growing but has since leveled off. In mid 1977 approximately 750,000 persons in the U.S. were working full-time less than 5 days a week. Though many employers are continuing to explore and adopt compressed workweek variations, there is a corresponding 4 to 15% discontinuance rate – approximately equal to new adoptions.[50]

Research findings indicate that the success of a compressed workweek schedule depends upon a variety of factors. Problems due to fatigue, increased complexity of work scheduling or employee scheduling, family and home conflicts, supervisory and communication problems are likely to occur.[51]

The compressed workweek is not specifically adopted by firms to appeal to older workers. In fact the literature suggests that the adoption of a compressed workweek may be unattractive to older workers. Balch suggests that the change to a compressed schedule may not appeal to older workers for the following reasons: "1) the older employee is likely to be conservative about any changes that influences his job, 2) The fatigue effect of a longer work day with longer intervals between rest periods threatens his ability to maintain performance comparable to younger workers, and 3) Fatigue toward the end of the day could make older employees more susceptible to accidents . . . with reduced recuperative powers, an element of double jeopardy may exist for older workers."[52]

Other studies on employee attitudes and experience with compressed workweeks indicate that compressed workweeks are more likely to appeal to younger workers than older workers – but industry, occupation, personal and firm specific factors are important influences on employee attitudes. A survey sample of full-time employed men found that the 4 day compressed workweek is more attractive to male workers who are young and desire more leisure time.[53] A study of a random sample of Oregon state employees found that young workers were more likely to favor the compressed workweek more than older workers. Of those 20 to 39 years of age, 81% favored the compressed schedule versus 49% of those 60 to 64 years of age. The most frequent reasons for opposition were fatigue and personal conflicts.[54] Another study of white collar workers' attitudes toward the 4 day 40 hour week found that workers aged 18 to 30 overwhelmingly favored the 4/40 while workers aged 51 to 70 overwhelmingly disliked it.[55]

In conclusion, existing studies indicate that older workers not currently working on a compressed workweek schedule are more likely to resist the change to a compressed workweek. Increased fatigue is the major reason workers expressed opposition to the longer working day. Among employees currently working a compressed workweek the effect of age on job satisfaction and attitudes toward the compressed workweek is less clear. Perhaps, older individuals actually working a compressed workweek find the fatigue factor to be offset by other benefits, such as increased leisure. Nevertheless, the available literature does indicate that the compressed workweek is less likely to find favor among older workers than younger workers.

The compressed workweek may aid in opening part-time jobs within a company. As firms adopt compressed schedules there is often a need for part-time positions to prevent the disruption of production schedules and customer services. The creation of such positions may allow older workers to phase more gradually into retirement. Employers may also take advantage of the older workers' experience and mature work habits and permit older workers to adjust their compressed work schedule to suit their individual needs. Schedules could be adopted which permit individual flexibility while completing certain specific work to be done within a specified period.[56]

OTHER ISSUES IN THE EMPLOYMENT OF OLDER WORKERS

Job Retraining, Promotion, and Voluntary Demotion

Other approaches to flexible retirement involve redirecting or redefining the careers of older employees. These approaches may include education to preserve workers' competence in their current jobs, in-house training and development to equip workers for career changes, retraining for jobs that may better suit the employees' interests and/or abilities, and modifications to the content of work performed.[57] In high technology industries, constantly changing technologies may require that workers be given training opportunities simply to prevent skill obsolescence.

Employer reluctance to invest in training of older workers is largely due to poor rates of anticipated return on their investment.[58] Opportunities to participate in new learning experiences generally decline as a person approaches retirement. Policies which do not reward the acquisition of new skills by older workers encourage retirement and fail to utilize the full productive capacities of a firm's work force. These low expectations are often based on the widespread belief that older individuals simply do not respond well to training and that retirement may preclude a proper return on the training investment. Consequently, job retraining to better equip workers for employment has often been unavailable to older workers. Arguments concerning the cost effectiveness of training older workers frequently ignore turnover rates for workers which differ by age, as well as the potential for lengthening the worklife of the older employees. Older workers, age 45 and over tend to stay on the same job longer than younger workers. In almost all cases, as age increases mobility decreases. The longer a worker is with one employer the less likely he or she is to move into another occupation.[59] Significantly lower turnover rates among older workers and their greater likelihood of staying in the same occupation, increase the chances that training investment will be recouped by the employer.

Returns on training investments in older workers have been found to be favorable. Belbin found that older trainees remained in their employment significantly longer than did younger graduates.[60] This finding was corroborated in work completed by Newsharn in 1969.[61] Strondorfer also found benefit-cost ratios of 200–300% in conjunction with the training of workers age 55, based upon a 10% discount rate.[62] If training further leads to the delay of retirement, rates of return would be even higher. These findings are corroborated in the experiences of a number of firms currently pursuing active training programs for older workers.

Another reason advanced for not retraining older workers cites the lower levels of education among older workers compared to younger labor force subgroups. The validity of this concern is questionable according to recent demographic statistics. The educational gap between younger and older workers has narrowed significantly in recent years. By 1990, the median years of education for workers aged 45 to 54 is projected to be 12.6, and 12.5 for those aged 55 to 64, compared to 12.7 for the total civilian labor force.[63] The relevance of years of formal education to the ability to perform on the job is also subject to question. For skilled workers "machine intuition" may be a more important prerequisite for a job than a college degree. The recent widespread and well-documented decline in achievement levels and literacy rates among high school graduates has also made formal education measures for younger workers less reliable as predictors of eventual job performance. Employers of machinists and other skilled workers, for example, are complaining that many younger workers lack the necessary literacy skills to read blueprints or manuals.

At the core of the argument against retraining older workers is the question of the decline in ability to learn new tasks as a person ages. Available research, while not conclusive, indicates that learning ability and intelligence do not necessarily decline with age. There are also reasons to believe that new training is complementary with previous training and that the prior experience of older workers may result in a decrease in the marginal cost of training with age.[64]

Possible relationships between age and the ability to learn have been the object of considerable interest. Recent research has found problem solving, number facility and verbal comprehension to be unaffected by age.[65] In general, research indicates that there are greater differences *within* groups of older *and* younger workers than *between* different age cohorts.[66] Green notes that a minimum of 20 research studies found no tendencies for skills relating to vocabulary, general information, judgment, or identifying similarities to drop before age 60.[67] Thurnin found flexibility and test performance unresponsive to age in the range between 19 and 56.[68] Haberlandt found no tendencies between ages 40 and 60 for loss of memory or learning ability. While learning curves for older subjects reflected a longer "start up" phase, by the end of the training, age differences had disappeared. Training in which time pressures are minimized and self-paced learning techniques are incorporated are particularly suited to older workers.[69] Although more information is needed on the differential validity of training methods by age, there is apparently no reason to anticipate lesser training success rates among older workers than among the younger elements of the labor force.

These findings would indicate that managers should examine workers' potential for training individually and not based on chronological age. Managers should also reassess training programs which limit opportunities for older workers and consider training programs which utilize methods, such as programmed teaching, which have been found to be effective in teaching older workers. A 55 year old potentially has many productive years to contribute to an employer. To the extent older workers are arbitrarily eliminated from training or educational programs, the organization is missing opportunities to utilize skills effectively.

Organizational policies regarding training and promotional opportunities may play an important role in reinforcing the popular belief that performance — especially for persons in high technology occupations — tends to decline as workers age. In a study of 2,500 design engineers and managers in 60 companies, Dalton and Thompson concluded that the "performance decline syndrome" was a symptom of discriminatory personnel practices rather than skill obsolescence.[70]

Myths concerning the older worker may be one of the primary barriers influencing employers' policies toward older workers. Generally the prevalent myths assume that as individuals age their abilities and productivity decline. Older workers, a very diverse group, are stereotyped into categories of incompetence.[71] Age stereotyping may result in employers developing policies or performing actions which encourage older workers to withdraw from the labor force. In a study of corporate managers, respondents were asked to make decisions regarding organizational and personnel problems. Two versions of a questionnaire were utilized equally; in one a 32 year old was the key individual in the problem situation and in the other it was a 61 year old. Although respondents indicated that they valued both younger and older workers, their responses indicated an age bias. The managers:

- Saw more difficulty in changing behavior of older employees.
- Did not attribute positive motives to older workers desiring retraining.
- Favored career development for younger workers, but not for older workers.
- Suggested by-passing the older worker rather than dealing with him directly.
- Saw the older workers as less likely to be promoted than younger workers.[71]

Thus, an intangible age bias — not acknowledged by the managers overtly — may present barriers to older employees. Beliefs that older employees have poorer health, lower productivity, rigid behavior, the inability to learn new skills, and higher accident rates may influence the employer to treat older and younger employees differently in terms of retention, hiring, promotion, evaluation and retraining. Personnel appraisal systems which emphasize qualities often associated with youth — such as aggressiveness or enthusiasm — may be subtly biased against older workers. Such evaluations may also work against older employees due to their emphasis on measurable quantities and lack of inclusion of equally important qualities, such as experience, which might favor older workers. The actions and evaluations of the employer may influence the employee to retire.[72]

Promotional Opportunities

Promotions are one of the most important rewards for work and provide an impetus for hope and motivation. Although few studies have examined the relationship between promotion and age, available data suggests that the opportunities for promotion and increasing job status may decrease with advancing age. Chinoy in a 1965 study of auto workers notes that promotions to foreman level were unusual after age 35.[73] Martin and Strauss also noted that age played an important part in promotions. In a more recent study of the age-promotion relationship across three time periods in a large corporation, Rosenbaum found that most promotions are allocated to youth and only a few promotions go to older employees. A gradual decline in opportunity occurs in the mid career years.[75] In a study of the older workers in a high technology firm, the authors found that four out of every ten respondents indicated that their opportunities for advancement were limited by their age. The lack, or perceived lack, of opportunity for promotion among older workers may result in a disengagement from work by older employees and an incentive for retirement.[76]

Voluntary Demotions/Transfers

The willingness of older workers to accept voluntary demotions or lateral transfers as alternatives to retirement, termination, or as the cost of obtaining more leisure time has not been well documented in the U.S. Although most retireees upon reentering the job market accept jobs with lower rates of pay or responsibility, the willingness of workers to accept demotion within the same organization, especially if it involves decreasing wages, is perhaps a less attractive alternative.[77]

American workers tend to believe that an exemplary work life is presumed to have only one direction — up.[78] Prevalent norms surrounding the concept of a successful worklife will need to be changed before the acceptance of downplacement or demotion is a common occurrence.

Present management policies are based on the assumption that working capacity increases or remains stable as workers age until retirement. At retirement the worker's capacity is presumably depleted.[79] Flexible career patterns that consider downward mobility to be as natural as upward mobility may be developed in the future. Further research on this sensitive issue needs to be undertaken to determine the feasibility of voluntary demotion programs as well as the conditions under which employees would be willing to accept such programs.

In *New Programs for Older Workers* the author notes that, "where demotion has worked successfully in this country, there have been three principles at work: mutual consent, time for exploration of alternatives and options, and the ability to transfer to another unit within the company to avoid peer pressure."[80] An additional and important factor is the affect of acceptance of the demotion on eventual retirement benefits.[81] An employee faced with the choice between retirement or the acceptance of demotion is likely to choose retirement if the demotion will reduce future pension benefits. An employee interested in continuing to work would then be eligible to collect pension benefits while seeking employment with a new employer.

In Denmark, the Danish Institute for Personnel Management (DIPM) conducted a 1978 study to determine how managers themselves perceived demotion.[83] The survey sampled Danish managers in companies in all industries with work forces which averaged 1,300 employees. Managers were asked the following question: "What would your reactions be if you were told that you would now be transferred to a different job, which it might be assumed would demand less competence and would be of a lower status than your present job." Possible reactions included:

1. Accept without question.
2. Reduce the work effort.
3. Work harder to be promoted again.
4. Seek other employment.

If a job title or a reduction in wages did not accompany the change, nearly 75% of the managers over 54 said they would accept the change in jobs. Younger executives, under 40, were much less likely to accept the change. When the change was accompanied by a lesser job title and a 10% salary reduction, 28% of those 55 and over (compared to 4% under 40) chose to accept the job without question. An additional 28% of those over 55 indicated they would accept the job with reduced work effort. When faced with the choice between accepting the downgraded job or early retirement, as many as 70% of the managers over 55 indicated they would accept the position.[84] At least for Danish managers, voluntary demotion would appear to be a viable alternative to early retirement.

The difference in labor markets, hiring practices, retirement benefits, and value systems between Denmark and the U.S. make it difficult to generalize from the findings of the Danish Study to U.S. workers. However, well-designed programs of voluntary demotion may be attractive to both older workers and employers in the U.S. in the future.

In a Pittsburgh study of managers and blue-collar workers aged 50 and above, Yitzchak Shkop found that the availability of hypothetical job modifications significantly altered the retirement plans of many employees. Managers in particular were likely to choose to remain in the organization if job modifications could be made. Although blue-collar workers were primarily interested in changing their time schedules, managers were interested in changing the content of their job. Almost one in three of the managers interested in job modifications desired special assignments. About one fifth of all the participants freely chose lower-level jobs as a desired option. Furthermore, when presented with the choice of staying in their current job with no modifications at all, accepting a lower-level job with modification, or leaving the organization, 27% of the respondents chose the lower-level job alternative. Almost one third of the managers chose this alternative.[85] Similar questions asked by the authors in a study of older workers in a high-technology firm indicated a willingness on the part of some workers to accept lower level positions. One fourth of the participants were interested in job modifications resulting in less responsible positions. Rather than continue on their current job or leave the organization, 16% were willing to accept a job with lower status and a lower salary.

Although limited in their scope, the findings from these two studies suggest that a number of American workers, particularly managers, would consider downgrading their position. This option certainly warrants further exploration. If one in five managers in a firm were willing to downgrade their position, the firm would have considerable flexibility in its management structure. If managers, in particular, are willing to step aside, the retention of older workers need not result in blocking career opportunities of younger workers. Similar studies, expanded to include other classifications of workers, should be done in the U.S. to obtain information on the feasibility of such programs.

CONCLUSION

Present personnel and remuneration policies are generally based on the assumption that workers are full-time employees until retirement at which time employment abruptly ceases. The changing composition of the labor force as well as demographic shifts leading to the greying of the American workforce, will require the development of new personnel and benefit policies to meet future needs. A reassessment of the structuring of work as well as remuneration should be undertaken by private and public sector policy-makers.

Control over one's work life and employment in the later years is likely to be a major "employee benefit" of the next decades. Increasing pressure against age discrimination combined with demographic changes and high inflation rates, may result in many older persons desiring to work full-time on flexible schedules, work part-time, or otherwise change the nature of their employment. Currently, few employers understand the need or even the existence of the problem, but future realities will require that the problem be addressed.

As new personnel options and remuneration packages are developed and implemented by employers, older workers will need to carefully consider the costs and benefits of the various options open to them. Present options are generally clear cut — employees must retire completely from employment to receive pension benefits under most plans. In the future innovative programs, such as those described in the preceding chapter, will require the careful examination of projected income flows based on differing assumptions regarding inflation rates, probable wage increases, changing pension benefit formulas and other factors to determine the optimal work and remunerative package for each worker based on individual preferences. For example, even assuming "retirement neutral" benefit packages, older workers must weigh their desires to work part-time against the increased potential of lay-offs or termination of part-time positions during recessionary periods. The effect of receiving pension benefits at Time 1 and switching to part-time reemployment may also result in a significant reduction in eventual retirement benefits when compared to the worker continuing in full-time employment receiving wage increases and accumulating further service credits until Time 2. Employers will need to supply individuals with sufficient information as well as technical assistance for them to make rational decisions based on different projections. Consequently, both employers and employees will need to apply sophisticated analyses to determine the impacts of new alternative job policies and remunerative packages.

FOOTNOTES

1. Peter F. Drucker. *Toward the Next Economics And Other Essays.* New York: Harper and Row, 1981, p. 133.
2. JoAnn Lublin. "Labor Pains: Effects of 'Baby Bust' Are Shrinking Ranks of Younger Workers." *Wall Street Journal,* September 10, 1981, p. 1.
3. Bureau of Labor Statistics. *New Labor Force Projections to 1990.* U.S. Department of Labor, Special Labor Force Report 197. Washington, D.C.: U.S. Government Printing Office, 1977.
4. Stanley Nollen. *New Patterns of Work.* New York: Work in America Institute Inc., 1979.
5. Shirley Rhine. *America's Aging Population: Issues Facing Business and Society.* New York: The Conference Board, Inc., 1980.
6. Ibid.
7. Lois Copperman. "Alternative Work Patterns in Private Firms," *The Personnel Administrator,* October 1979.
8. Nollen, op. cit.

9. Stanley Nollen. "What is Happening to Flexitime, Flexitour, Gliding Time, the Variable Day, Permanent Part-Time Employment and the Four-Day Week? The Changing Workplace," *Across the Board.* New York: The Conference Board, Inc., April 1980.
10. Stanley Nollen, Brenda B. Eddy, and Virginia H. Martin, "Permanent Part-Time Employment: The Manager's Perspective," School of Business Administration, Georgetown University, Washington, D.C. 1977, p. 11.
11. Ibid, p. 12-13.
12. Ibid, p. 70.
13. Nollen, 1979, op. cit.
14. Ibid.
15. Allan Cohen and Herman Gadon. *Alternative Work Schedules: Integrating Individual and Organizational Needs.* Massachusetts: Addison-Wesley Publishing Co., 1978.
16. Nollen, 1979, op. cit.
17. William B. Werther, Jr. "Mini-Shifts: An Alternative to Overtime, *Personnel Journal,* March 1976.
18. Ibid.
19. Susie Anschell. *Potential for Semi-Retirement in Public Agencies.* Seattle: University of Washington, 1980.
20. Ibid.
21. Elizabeth Meier. *Implications for Employment.* Washington, D.C.: The National Council on Aging, 1976.
22. Johnson and Higgins. *1979 Study of American Attitudes Toward Pensions and Retirement,* conducted by Harris Associates, N.Y. 1979.
23. Herbert S. Parnes, Gilbert Nestel, Thomas N. Chirikos, Thomas N. Daymont, Frank L. Mott, Donald O. Parsons and Associates. *From the Middle to the Later Years: Longitudinal Studies of the Preretirement and Postretirement Experiences of Men.* Columbus, Ohio: Ohio State University, 1979.
24. Anschell, op. cit.
25. Ibid.
26. Stephen R. McConnell, Dorothy Fleisher, Carolyn E. Usher, and Barbara Hade Kaplan. *Alternative Work Options for Older Workers.* Andrus Gerontology Center, University of Southern California, 1980.
27. Ibid.
28. Ibid.
29. Ibid.
30. Lois Copperman, Fred D. Keast, and Douglas C. Montgomery. "Older Workers and Part-Time Work Schedules," *Personnel Administrator,* October 1981.
31. Ibid.
32. Anschell, op. cit.
33. Ibid.
34. McConnel et al., op. cit.
35. Copperman et al., op. cit.
36. Ibid.

37. Cohen and Gadon, op. cit.
38. Ibid.
39. Nollen, 1979, op. cit.
40. Nollen, 1980, op. cit.
41. Ibid.
42. William Glueck. "Changing Hours of Work: A Review and Analysis of the Research," *Personnel Administrator,* March 1979.
43. Copperman et al., op. cit.
44. Nollen, 1980, op. cit.
45. McConnel et al., op. cit.
46. Ibid.
47. Glueck, op. cit.
48. Cohen and Gadon, op. cit.
49. Ibid.
50. Ibid.
51. Nollen and Martin, op. cit.
52. B. W. Balch. "The Four-Day Week and the Older Worker," *Personnel Journal,* December 1974.
53. Robert E. Allen and Douglas K. Hawes. "Attitudes Toward Work, Leisure and the Four Day Workweek," *Human Resources Management,* Spring 1979.
54. Martin Kenny. "Public Employee Attitudes Toward the Four Day Week," *Public Personnel Management,* April 1974.
55. Thomas A. Mahoney, Jerry M. Newmand and Peter J. Frost. "Workers Perception of the Four Day Week," *California Management Review,* Fall 1975.
56. Balch, op. cit.
57. James Walker and Harriet L. Lazer. *The End of Mandatory Retirement,* New York: John Wiley and Sons, Inc., 1978.
58. Elizabeth Meier and Elizabeth Kerr. "Capabilities of Middle-aged and Older Workers: A Survey of the Literature," *Industrial Gerontology,* Summer 1976. Also, Ernst Stromsdorfer. *A Cost Benefit Analysis of Retraining,* Ph.D. Dissertation, St. Louis: Washington University, 1970.
59. James Byrne. "Occupational Mobility of Workers," *Monthly Labor Review,* February 1975.
60. R. M. Belbin. *Training Methods for Older Workers,* in Irvin Sober, *Employment: Background and Issues.* Washington, D.C.: White House Conference on Aging, March 1971.
61. Nollen, op. cit.
62. Stromsdorfer, op. cit.
63. Ibid.
64. Ibid.
65. Jeffrey Sonnenfeld. "Dealing with the Aging Work Force," *Harvard Business Review,* November–December 1978.
66. Belbin, op. cit.
67. Russell Green. "Age, Intelligence and Learning," *Industrial Gerontology,* Fall 1973.

68. Fred Thumin. "MMPI As a Function of Chronological Age," *Industrial Gerontology*, June 1969.
69. Karl F. Haberlandt. "Learning, Memory and Age," *Industrial Gerontology*, Fall 1973.
70. G. W. Dalton and P. H. Thompson. "Accelerating Adolescence of Older Engineers," *Harvard Business Review*, 1971.
71. David Peterson. *The Older Worker: Myths and Realities*. Los Angeles: Andrus Gerontology Center, USC, 1980.
72. Ibid.
73. Ely Chinoy. *Automobile Workers and the American Dream*. New York: Random House, 1955.
74. N. H. Martin and A. L. Strauss. "Patterns of Mobility within Industrial Organizations," in W. Lloyd Warner and N. H. Martin, *Industrial Man*. New York: Harper, 1959.
75. James E. Rosenbaum. "Organizational Career Mobility: Promotion Chances in a Corporation during Periods of Growth and Contraction," *American Journal of Sociology*, July 1979.
76. Ibid.
77. McConnel et al., op. cit.
78. Beverly Jacobson. *Young Programs for Older Workers*. New York: Van Nostrand Reinhold Co., 1980.
79. Ibid.
80. Ibid.
81. Ibid.
82. Copperman and Keast, op. cit.
83. Jacobson, op. cit.
84. Ibid.
85. Yitzchak Shkop. *The Effects of Providing Various Options for Continued Employment in the Organization of Patterns of Retirement Decisions*, Doctoral Thesis University of Pittsburgh, 1980.

4
Compensation:
Examining Remuneration

INTRODUCTION

Discussions of employment which treat work separately from remuneration inevitably incur the risk of ignoring the close linkages between the two. The relationship is highlighted in Webster's definition of employment — "work in which one's labor or services are paid for by an employer."[1] For older as well as younger workers, compensation is a key factor in labor force participation rates.

The compositions of work and remuneration are subject to considerable independent variation. The flexitime schedule identified in the previous chapter, for example, offers the employer the opportunity to tailor one aspect of employment — the structure of requisite time commitments — to the needs of employees without undertaking any alterations in the remunerative package offered to workers. The offering of part-time options, on the other hand, necessarily requires complementary alterations to the pay package. Other practices, such as "temporary retirement," "tapering off" of work after the normal retirement age, and "regular full-time work after retirement"[2] demand innovation both in employment practice and remunerative strategy.

In general, remunerative packages bear one of three relations to the design of the job itself in the context of innovative employment practices.

- The redesigned work may be offered on its own merits, with no alterations in the remunerative package.
- The redesigned work may be offered in conjunction with complementary alterations to the remunerative package.
- The work itself may be continued without re-design, but remunerative packages may be developed which offer more appeal to a specific class of worker.

While the concept of tailoring remunerative packages to the preferences of older workers has received little attention in the literature — certainly less than have the work-related issues which are discussed in the preceding chapter — a number of employers have developed policies which are innovative and which appear to be effective in altering the retirement behavior of workers.

Compensatory practices are a valid focus of attention in the analysis of older worker labor force participation. Although the choice to withdraw from the labor force is voluntary, its timing is influenced by the anti-work biases of our retirement system, which themselves are outgrowths of the compensatory practices associated with the work place. With the exception of compulsory retirement which is now legally enforceable only at ages which make it irrelevant for most, no element of the employment system actually removes the individual from employment. Rather, prevalent policies and practices create conditions which influence workers to remove themselves as a result of rational decisionmaking. It is these elements of remunerative strategies which will be discussed here, along with alternative approaches which have been suggested and are actually in practice among firms seeking to reverse the prevalent pattern of early retirement.

This chapter will be comprised of three broad sections. The first will delineate in broad terms a number of fundamental issues and relationships which are important in the analysis of remunerative strategies and older workers. The second discussion will address various components of the remunerative package, emphasizing actual or potential impacts on the labor force participation of older workers. Skeletal descriptions of each practice will be provided highlighting those characteristics which might influence older individuals into or out of the labor force. Finally, the chapter will conclude with a broad discussion of how the discrete components of a remunerative strategy interact, and how they could relate to efforts to influence older workers to remain on the job.

The generation of successful remunerative practices is contingent upon a sound understanding of how the pay packages relate to the job and, more specifically, how older workers as a group relate to the pay package. The text which follows is designed to highlight these relationships.

BACKGROUND

Compensation is the most universal linkage between employees and workers, yet it is an association which is clouded by complex relationships borne of countless bodies of law and tax policy, by the policies and goals of millions of individual employers, and by variations in the aspirations of workers. Thus, while it is reasonable to assume that a more highly valued pay package is "better" than one of lesser value, it may be questionable to assume that increases should come as additions to take-home pay or the addition of dental insurance to the fringe benefit package. These issues notwithstanding, it is possible to identify a range of "facts" which relate to remuneration, and these constitute the focus of the discussion which follows.

Remuneration is comprised of two components:

- Periodic monetary compensation. More generally termed salary, wage, commission, bonus, or costs profit sharing, this form of remuneration is paid in a highly liquid form and generally on a regular basis.
- Fringe or welfare benefits. Fringe or welfare benefits (the terms will be employed interchangeably throughout this discussion) are in-kind payments in the form of insurance coverages, or, in the case of pension related mechanisms, conditional promissory obligations payable at a later date. While not paid in cash at the time work is performed, these benefits can be valued in a monetary sense and, if not disposable income per se, they may nonetheless be assessed in terms of expenses or savings which needn't be sustained presently by the worker.

A number of broad issues define the role of compensation packages in the development of effective policies targeted at older workers. In very general terms, these may be summarized as follows:

- Remuneration has the effect of motivating workers. This topic has been the subject of considerable discussion. In general, rates of remuneration have a bearing on worker attitudes, motivation, and performance.[3] Investigators researching this topic, however, tend to examine only monetary wages, or to operationalize compensation solely in terms of monetary value. Discussions of the systematic differences which exist in workers' valuation of non-monetary compensation, and which distinguish the value between various forms of monetary payment are generally unavailable.

- Systematic differences exist in workers' valuations of individual components of the compensation package, and some of these differences are associated with age. Chapman and Otterman[4] suggest that, " . . . a reward motivates only if it satisfies an individual's needs." To the extent that a remunerative package entails benefits which do not address needs — or address them to a lesser degree than other, alternative benefits — the expense to the employer is not likely to generate maximal returns in worker motivation. If individual needs co-vary with age, and there is reason to believe that they do, it is reasonable to anticipate that workers' valuations of benefits will change as individuals advance through the lifecycle. Research has shown, for example, that older workers attach significantly greater importance to pension and retirement related welfare benefits than do their younger colleagues, and that they are less enthusiastic about a range of other benefits.[5,6,7] Assumptions of homogeneity among workers with respect to the valuation of compensation packages are generally not supported by research findings. A number of factors suggest that employers must begin to alter remunerative packages if they wish to obtain maximum productive return for their benefit dollars and/or encourage older workers to remain on the job.

- Employers are not able to indefinitely expand the scope and depth of compensation packages offered to workers. The typical large American firm spends amounts equal to 35 to 40% of wage and salary expense on fringe benefits:[8] this compares to a similar figure of 7% as recently as 1945. This expansion in expense reflects both the broadening of coverages over that period, and an increase in the costs of providing individual coverages. In this context, it is to the advantage of employers to maximize the value perceived by workers in return for the expense entailed in providing a remunerative package, a concept referred to by Koralik as "efficiency of benefit expenditures."[9]

- Many older workers have access to income sources other than earnings. Eligibility for income from sources related to retirement in effect diminishes the financial rewards available through employment. In a very real sense, eligibility for retirement adds to the opportunity cost associated with work. Earnings among retirement eligible workers are realistically valued only to the extent that they exceed pension related income foregone, plus any favorable impacts on subsequent income streams derived from continued employment. The financial ability to elect early retirement has been cited as the most prominent factor in the decline of labor force participation rates among men over age 60.[10, 11, 12, 13]

- The likelihood of individual labor force participation varies directly with the value of compensation to be derived through work. Various public and private policies currently have a direct effect on the amount of disposable income derived by older individuals from employment. Three primary factors may have a major impact on employment decisions. First, those who are eligible for social security benefits are actually or potentially affected by the social security retirement test which directly penalizes workers who earn over a specified minimum amount. The second influence on labor force participation is also related to the social security program. Earned income from employment is subject to a number of taxes while social security benefits available to retired workers are tax exempt. Finally, most pension plans require that the worker leave the employer providing pension benefits before benefits can be paid. Because older workers frequently encounter difficulty in obtaining re-employment,[14, 15, 16] this enforced period of joblessness can be expected to contribute to labor force withdrawal.

- Employment among older workers constitutes not only a means of generating current income, but in many cases also represents the means by which the quality of later retirement can be most effectively improved. It is not reasonable to anticipate that the worker who has worked beyond the normal retirement age has turned a cold shoulder to retirement: it is more realistic to suspect that retirement will simply begin at a later time or perhaps in a different fashion. Through savings opportunities, wage increases, extended pension accruals (where offered), and continued social security participation, it is very possible for the worker to achieve a more satisfactory current standard of living through continued work while simultaneously improving the standard of living which will subsequently be realized in later years.

These observations constitute a preface to the remainder of this chapter. In a number of very important ways, older workers are different from their younger colleagues. Moreover, older workers who are able to retire comfortably — or who soon will be — are different than those of similar age for whom retirement is not financially feasible. These differences can bear important implications for policy implemented by government and, just as importantly, for individual employers. The remainder of the chapter discusses the compensation practices through which these differences between workers — based largely on age-related phenomena — gain their significance.

Remunerative Practices

The differentiation of compensation between earnings and fringe benefits is not of much significance to most observers at first glance: the pay package is, after all, worth what it is worth and, in any event, there's not much to be done about it. As the length of this chapter may suggest, however, this issue is more complex than it appears. A number of workers are able to exercise some control over the timing and tax liabilities generated by their earnings. Tax codes at all levels treat fringe benefits more favorably than earnings: in part due to recognition of this fact, the social security administration incorporates into its revenues projections a steady transfer of value from monetary to fringe compensation. Additionally, research has shown that age is a factor in workers' preference for pay options and fringe benefits. Finally, age and retirement/employment status are major factors in the value of remuneration earned by workers. These factors constitute the discussion which follows. Monetary compensation, fringe benefits, and retirement policies, will be addressed in that order. Finally, a brief discussion will relate these pay-related topics to other elements of the employment package.

Monetary Compensation. All earnings mechanisms share two important characteristics. First, they are distributed in a highly liquid form on a regular basis. Second, with few exceptions they are subject to income and social security taxation during the fiscal period in which they are earned. The taxation of earned income has important implications for retirement behavior. To the extent that income is taxed, nominal rates of pay exceed actual "take-home" pay. If earnings are subject to taxation while alternative forms of income are not, the relative value of the untaxed income source is enhanced. This is an important issue among older workers since social security benefits are tax free. Most workers achieve their highest earnings in the years preceding retirement.[17] Thus, they may be subject to their highest lifetime tax rates at exactly the time when retirement becomes a viable alternative.

Deferred Earnings. Deferred earnings programs, such as pensions, permit workers to delay the actual receipt of work-generated income until a later time. This practice defers tax liability until the earnings are actually received by the individual. If tax liabilities are less at the time of receipt than at the time of the work which generated the income, the individual realizes a net reduction in tax liability and an equivalent increase in the value of take-home pay. A second deferred earnings mechanism is The Individual Retirement Account (IRA's). IRA's permit workers to delay paying taxes on a specified percentage of their annual income which is placed in a qualified retirement savings plan. Another mechnism is the deferred compensation plan available to workers in the public and non-profit enterprises. Under this program, tax liabilities up to 20% of earnings are deferred until the moneys and accumulated interest are withdrawn.

The implementation of deferred earnings programs is limited by federal and state legislation. Individual employers may take advantage of available opportunities to defer taxation of earnings at their own discretion. Such programs may be increasingly attractive to employers of a greying workforce.

Other Compensation Practices. More appropriately within the auspice of the employer is the pay package developed in conjunction with alternative employment programs. As suggested in the preceding chapter, there is considerable reason to anticipate that when presented with part-time alternatives ranging between the polar choices of full-time work in the same job or no work at all, a number of older employees will choose to continue on the job in a reduced capacity in terms of responsibility or time commitment.

It is less clear whether workers are willing to accept reductions in income in order to exercise these options. One recent study of older workers at Lockheed Corporation and The City of Los Angeles found little enthusiasm for alternative work options including diminished responsibilities if participation was to be accompanied by reductions in income. These researchers reported that while fully 28% of respondents were attracted to the idea of diminished full-time responsibilities as a means of extending the work life, only 8% expressed a willingness to absorb a 10% reduction in earnings in conjunction with such a change, and only 6% would accept a 25% pay reduction. Similarly, while 39% of respondents expressed interest in converting to part-time work, only 7% were interested if forced to bear a proportionate reduction in income.

The possibility of augmenting earnings with pension payments, however, offers promise to the employer seeking to address these issues. McConnell et al.[18] found that if the proportionately reduced earnings were augmented with pro-rated pension payments, 39% of surveyed workers were interested in the option of shifting to part-time work and, concurrently, delaying total retirement. An investment firm studied by Copperman and Keast,[19] implemented a similar plan by disbursing accumulated deferred profit sharing funds at the 65th birthday rather than at retirement. This practice permitted qualified workers to draw income simultaneously from earnings and pensions. Only 1 worker had retired in the 2 years preceding the study, though 32 of the firm's 300 workers were over the age of 65.

Earnings from reduced work may also be augmented through social security. Where 1982 earnings remain below $6,000 for those over 65, social security benefits are not affected by earnings, and net work-generated income escapes the 50% marginal tax associated with the retirement test. Those over age 72 are not subject to the retirement test restrictions. In a study of innovative employment practices, Copperman and Keast[20] found an acute awareness of the social security earnings test among part-time workers, and explicit tailoring of earnings so as to avoid losses in benefits. For these workers, however, social security benefits may offset a major proportion of the earnings lost through conversion to part-time work. Moreover, the progressive tax rates of the Internal Revenue Service (IRS) code in conjunction with the tax exemption of social security benefits promotes part-time work. However, the promise offered through social security is limited in its appeal. The 65 year old worker maintaining a part-time employment schedule of 1,000 hours per year can earn only up to $6.00 per hour and escape the retirement test. Above that level, earnings subject the worker to losses of social security benefits which deteriorate the monetary incentives associated with extended employment.

In summary, two influences associated with monetary compensation are likely to affect the labor force participation of older workers.

- The availability of deferred earnings programs, which can favorably influence the quality of later retirement are likely to prolong the working career. Tax codes, however, bar employers from pursuing this practice other than through pension-related programs.
- Older workers' enthusiasm in prolonging their worklives through participation in reduced levels of employment appears to be contingent upon the availability of supplemental sources of income not related to present work commitments. Employers augmenting earnings with moneys generated from pension sources have achieved success in delaying their workers' retirements, and surveys have shown workers to be amenable to this approach. Further, where workers age 65 to 72 earn less than $6.00 (in 1982) per hour benefits paid through social security can be employed as supplements to earnings. The retirement test, however, precludes this mechanism from directly benefitting workers of higher skills and pay levels: above this rate of pay, workers must either bear some reduction in take home pay due to the impacts of the retirement test, or must reduce their work involvement to less than 1,000 hours per year. Restrictions on social security beneficiaries younger than 65 are more severe: retirement test for this group in 1982 is below $4,400. As a result, these social security recipients can only engage in normal

part-time work (1,000 hours per year) at wages less than $4.40 per hour before the retirement test affects their income or labor market involvement.

Fringe Benefits

Fringe, or welfare benefits constitue a diverse range of non-monetary compensations available to workers by or through an employer. Common fringe benefits include pensions, a variety of insurance coverages commonly including medical, disability, life, and dental, and a host of others such as paid time off the job in the form of vacations, holidays and sabbatical leaves, and possibly even access to such mass-marketed products as auto insurance at rates lower than are otherwise available.

While capable of being valued in monetary terms through comparison with similar products or services on the market, fringe benefits are provided "in kind" or in the case of retirement benefits, as conditional promissory obligations. The provision of fringe benefits is in a very real sense promoted by tax codes, which have exempted from personal income taxation the non-monetary benefits provided by the employer.

The period since 1930 has been one of steady expansion in the provision of non-monetary benefits offered through the workplace. One authority notes that 7% of payroll expended on non-monetary benefits by the typical employer in 1945 had grown to 35 to 40% in 1978.[21] There are two components to this expansion: the breadth of or number of programs offered to the worker, and their cost.

Through the mid-1960s, increases in benefit costs were largely a product of benefit expansion.[22] Since that time, however, inflation-fueled increases in the costs of individual coverages has emerged as a factor of independent importance. One authority notes that, "the trend toward liberalizing benefits seems to be at a plateau. Not so the case of benefits' costs." Increases in costs are acknowledged to be generating two sorts of impacts. First, as noted above, there is increasing resistance to the expansion of benefit offerings. Second, increased costs are generating heightened interest among personnel officers in realizing the greatest returns possible from benefit expenditures.

The diversity of fringe benefits offered by employers precludes detailed discussion of all possible alternatives. Accordingly, specific attention will be restricted to pensions, and to life, health, and disability insurance. Paid time off the job, addressed in the preceding chapter, will be mentioned here as well. Other aspects of fringe benefits will be addressed in general terms with an emphasis on those fringe benefits which can be expected to influence labor force participation among older workers.

Any discussion of labor force participation among older workers must also include a consideration of the Old Age and Survivors' Income (OASI) programs of the Social Security Administration. While not an employer-provided benefit per se, these are nonetheless employment related pension programs with very real influences on the employment options and practices of older workers. The following section presents a discussion of benefit preferences as they relate to older workers.

Benefit Preferences

Improvement of returns on the fringe benefit dollar is an issue of increasing interest to employees and employers alike — age-related preferences in fringe benefits will grow in importance in coming decades. In the context of a homogeneous labor force and short time horizons, the matching of employer selections of benefits with workers' preferences is a relatively simple issue to resolve. Research has shown, however, that labor forces are seldom homogeneous with respect to benefit preferences, and that while the time horizons associated with workers' benefit preferences may well be short, the length of the periods necessary for funding certain benefits — pensions, in particular — is far longer and therefore not conducive to short term employee participation. Both factors relate to age.

Chapman and Otterman,[23] in a survey of employees for a large industrial employer, found that when questioned about preferences in how a 5% expansion in benefits might be spent, those over age 50 were significantly more likely than their younger colleagues to identify earlier retirement and higher pension benefits. Younger workers were more likely to identify such options as the 4 day week and dental protection. Age was not found to be a factor in preferences for lengthened vacations, pay increases, and shorter work days. Another study, using 1,000 employees of the State of California as a sample, found that older workers were six times more likely to voluntarily expend fringe benefit dollars on retirement-related programs than were younger workers.[24] A third survey found similar preferences in a sample of office workers,[25] and a fourth found that older workers would prefer to contribute more to their pensions than possible under prevailing conditions.[26]

Flexible Benefits

One approach to reconciling these differences in employee preferences is the "cafeteria-style" of benefits in which workers select the benefits in which their fringe expenditures will be made. Workers are given a package of benefits that includes "basic" and "optional" items. The basic package might include modest medical coverage, life insurance equal to one year's salary, moderate pension contributions and vacation time commensurate with years of service. Employees then use their credits to choose among additional benefits such as high employer contributions to retirement fund, dental care, or additional medical coverage. Cafeteria plans offer employers the opportunity to maximize the correlation between employee priorities and benefits, and offer employees maximal flexibility in the employment of resources expended in their behalf. Proponents of this approach to benefit provision suggest that cafeteria plans offer maximal returns to the organization at "virtually no cost to the organization."[27] The plans have the advantage of allowing companies to give the illusion of providing employees with more benefits. Flexible benefits have been shown to reduce turnover in one large company and to serve as a good recruitment tool.

Yet cafeteria plans have not achieved widespread use. One recent survey found that only 1.2% of responding companies had implemented cafeteria plans.[28] This low rate of acceptance suggests that total flexibility in benefit selection bears problems as well as promises. Flexibility in benefit selection received a setback due to a 1974 tax law which required the taxation of all benefits chosen by employees. Recent revisions in the law have revived employer's interest in the program. Aside from taxation issues two primary obstacles to the adoption of flexible benefits have been identified. One problem identified above relates to the incompatability of short-range benefit

preferences and the long-term funding requirements of various benefits — especially pensions. One researcher found that given total
flexibility, only 9.1% of surveyed workers under age 25 would expend
benefit resources on pension coverage,[29] yet early participation is an
important element in the funding of benefits which increase in importance to the worker as the worker ages. Consequently, a minimally
acceptable pension contribution must be included as part of the basic
package.

Other problems with cafeteria-style benefits are related to the costs.
Under most plans, employees can readjust their benefit packages once
a year. Where employees can exercise short-term flexibility in benefit
selection, the costs associated with benefit administration and book-
keeping necessarily increase.[30] A second, longer-term source of cost
increases is associated with "adverse selection," a process where only
those most in need of a coverage are those who procure it. This
process increases the frequency and costs of claims, and ultimately
elevates the premiums charged by the insurer.

Mid-range approaches to flexibility in benefit selection are available. Koralik[31] cites the "9 per cent plan," in which employees
exercise limited flexibility in conjunction with a core of mandatory
benefits. Other companies offer selections between alternative programs of similar scope. Hewitt Associates[32] reports that while close
to half of responding companies offer a selection between group
medical coverages and HMO's, only 5.4% offer options between cash
and deferred profit sharing, and only 6.4% allow workers to select
between cash and vacations.

While flexibility in benefit selection has not yet gained wide popu-
larity among employers, the practice nonetheless offers potential
reward in the rentention of older workers. It is simply not consistent
with maximizing efficiencies in benefit expenditures or with the needs
of workers to extend family medical coverage, for example, to workers
whose families are grown. Older workers, shown empirically to orient
strongly to retirement-related benefits, would likely value more highly
the extension of benefits which could improve life after retirement.
This preference is reflected in a 1979 survey which found widespread
interest among older workers in contributing more to their pension
funds. Dental coverage after retirement, for example, might generate
greater interest than would a number of alternatives. Similarly

accelerated contributions to pensions — perhaps even freedom for employee contributions to pension plans, may well generate greater interest. While no empirical research has focused on these issues, the ability to favorably influence post-retirement standards of living is likely to influence workers to remain on the job.

1978 Amendments to the Age Discrimination in Employment Act

The legal requirements which govern the extension of benefits to older workers have received wide coverage in the literature in the wake of the 1978 Amendments to the Age Discrimination in Employment Act (ADEA). Known primarily for the extension of the earliest permissible mandatory retirement age to 70 from 65, these amendments further addressed the terms of employment offered to older workers, including fringe benefit coverages. In general, the amendments provide that with the exception of pension programs, the fringe benefits extended to older workers must be similar to those offered younger employers, either by virtue of value or cost.

The actual application of this broad rule, however, is subject to considerable variation when individual benefits are addressed. Three benefits, in particular, have generated considerable discussion, health insurance, life insurance, and disability insurance.

- *Life Insurance.* Life insurance available to older workers must match in cost that provided for younger employees. While reductions in insurance value are permitted, these reductions must reflect the actuarial increases in the costs of providing coverage to members of this age group. This guideline allows an 8% per annum decrement in insurance value after age 65, or a 35% reduction for the bracketed, 5 year span from 66 to 70.
- *Health Insurance.* The availability of Medicare offers employers a potential saving in the provision of health insurance to workers over 65. While the health insurance package must be consistent with that offered other employees, older workers' coverage can be structured so as to incorporate Medicare Parts A and B. This policy demands that employers pay the premiums of Part B, a requirement which has generated a number of mechanisms among employers for the reimbursement of workers.

- *Disability Insurance.* The treatment of disability insurance has become an issue because of the potential for older disabled workers to stretch their dependency on disability payments and delay the receipt of retirement and pension-based income sources. Disability insurance coverage for older workers is required to match in benefits that offered to younger employees in one of two ways. First, employees disabled before age 60 may draw benefits through age 65. Second, those disabled after age 60 are eligible for benefits equal to the average duration of paid younger workers.

The ADEA Guidelines are intended to insure coverage for older workers while simultaneously protecting employers and older workers alike from the possible higher costs of employment of older persons.

It is clear that employers have developed considerable variation in their approaches to benefit packages for older workers, with a substantial minority exceeding minimally acceptable guidelines as established by legislation and administrative regulations.

The provision of life insurance reflects the greatest inter-employer variation, with much lesser differences encountered among other coverages.

Much less differentiation is reflected in the means by which benefits are selected. Very few firms offer their workers the opportunity to choose the benefits they are providing.

Retirement Programs

Early descriptions of the role of social security employed a metaphorical reference to a three-legged stool which continues to apply today. The horizontal member of the stool, the individual's support in retirement, was — and is — based on income streams from three sources, each of which comprises one leg of the stool. One of these legs represents individual savings. The second reflects private pensions, offered through the place of work. Finally, the third leg consists of the social security programs. Though none of these three legs could individually support the individual, the three acting together could provide a suitable standard of living. While the first leg cited above — individual savings — will not be addressed in this discussion, the latter two are both derived through employment and therefore merit considerable attention: the fact that each generates very real influences on the retirement behavior of individuals makes their inclusion mandatory.

Private Pensions

The first American private pension was introduced in 1875 by the American Express Company. While primarily a source of disability income, this fringe benefit nonetheless heralded an era of rapid growth in pensions. By 1930, private pension coverage had been extended to 2.7 million members of the labor force — an unprecedented number — and increases in coverage have been virtually continuous since. Three events can be credited with the increased rates of expansion in pension coverage realized by American workers. The first was the passage into law of the Old Age Insurance program in 1935, and the subsequent provision of survivors' benefits and, in 1956, the addition of disability coverage. The second major factor in the expansion of pension coverage involved the wage-price controls implemented during World War II which, while limiting the salaries and wages which could be paid workers, did not extend these limitations to pension contributions. The third major influence was the 1948 decision by the National Labor Relations Board which recognized pension benefits as a legitimate issue in collective bargaining: from that beginning, organized labor has become a major force in the expansion and liberalization of pension coverage.

The influence of retirement income plans on the employment behavior of retirable workers in large measure reflects the provisions which are written into each individual plan. These provisions, however, tend to be repeated with considerable frequency from plan to plan, so that their effects can be widespread in spite of the employer-specific ramifications of each individual plan.

The term "pension plan" is a general reference which encompasses a considerable range of financial mechanisms designed to yield post-retirement income.

Pension programs can be differentiated from other fringe benefits in two ways.

First, where other forms of welfare benefits are paid in kind and are essentially consumed during the or shortly after the period in which they are earned, pension contributions constitute a monetary obligation on the part of the employer. More specifically, pensions may be likened to promissory financial instruments, payable upon the completion by the employee of a number of conditions. Typically among these conditions are participation of sufficient length in the program to qualify for the payment of accrued moneys (vesting), attainment of the age at which benefits are first payable, and generally the cessation of work for the company or companies sponsoring the pension plan which will disburse benefits.

Second, primary pensions are unique among welfare benefits – even other forms of pensions – in being excluded from the provisions set forth in the 1978 ADEA amendments which call for parity in the costs of provision of benefits to workers of all ages.

Seven types of pension mechanisms predominate among current offerings. At a very general level of analysis, these conform to one of funding principles. Defined benefit programs, which alone constitute the first group, are payable at retirement in scheduled amounts which are determined as functions of earnings and length of service: contributions to the fund are determined by the pension's potential costs in benefits. Other types of pensions, which fall into the second group, operate on the reverse principle in that ultimate benefits are determined by the amount of contributions set aside during the employee's period of coverage. Both groups can operate under provisions for employer and/or employee funding, though employer funding is more prevalent than is employee funding. Funding issues and the incentives to retirement associated with pensions are subject to considerable variation between the different approaches, so that specific descriptions of each are appropriate.

Defined benefit programs are provided through employers or other employment-related parties such as labor unions. In a defined benefit pension plan the employees are promised a fixed and determinable benefit at a specified age. Usually the promised benefit is tied to the employee's earnings, or length of service, or both. Since the primary goal of a retirement plan is to provide future retirement income for employees, the most effective plans are those which are available for long periods of benefit accumulation. The defined benefit plan is most successful for long-term employees and allows the employer to develop a program to achieve certain retirement income goals. Long service employees may base retirement plans on a known level of pension benefits. The three formulas presented below provide examples of benefit calculations utilized by employers to determine ultimate benefits:*

- Final Pay Pension — the most commonly utilized formula: 1.5% of the employee's final five year average earnings

  times

  years of service

  minus

  one-half of employee's primary social security benefit.
- Flat Benefit Pension — frequently utilized in union negotiated plans — $15 a month per year of service.
- Career Pay Pension — 1% of the employee's earnings up to the social security wage base

  plus

  2% of earnings in excess of social security wage base for each year of plan participation.[33]

The level of benefits available under the final pay pension formula is particularly sensitive to changes in wage rates during the years directly preceding retirement.

Until the 1973 passage of The Employee Retirement Income Security Act (ERISA), defined benefit programs were distinguishable from other forms of pension coverage by two characteristics: First, assets invested in pension programs remained the property of the sponsoring party, and, second, liabilities to the pension funds were not considered current until the worker's actual retirement. These characteristics led to the failure of many pension plans through the bankruptcies of sponsoring employers or through other problems. With requirements for full funding, for minimally acceptable investment procedures, for insurance of pension benefits through the Pension Benefit Guaranty Corporation, and for minimally acceptable vesting provisions, ERISA removed many of the pitfalls of defined benefit programs which became apparent during the 1960's. ERISA, however, ultimately generated another sort of impact on defined benefit plans. In

---

*Dollar figures and percentages are hypothetical.

addressing defined benefit plans only, ERISA generated a number of minimally acceptable practices which applied only to this type of plan.

In particular, the establishment of age 65 as the maximum acceptable normal retirement age, after which pension participation was no longer necessary, established a practice which carries over to the period after the extension of protected status of workers to age 70. While workers cannot now be mandatorily retired until age 70 (a product of the 1978 ADEA amendments) neither must they be covered under primary pension plans after the age of 65 (a product of ERISA). Since these plans extend to a large proportion of workers, the potential to lose that portion of the remunerative package previously represented by pension contributions and adjustment constitutes a widely influential disincentive to work among those over 65. Three aspects of pension participation are affected.

- The benefits due a worker at the normal retirement age need not be increased if the worker continued on the job past that age, even though the total value of the pension decreases through reductions in the duration of retirement.
- Service beyond the normal retirement age need not be credited in the determination of retirement benefit levels.
- Increases in earnings generated after the normal retirement age need not be included in calculations of average earnings for the purpose of benefit computations.

Freezing pension benefits encourages workers to retire. Although by continuing to work an employee may still have access to other company provided fringe benefits, their after-tax income may be only equal or slightly above the after-tax income they would receive from their combined pension and social security benefits. In addition to the monetary penalties, the combined effect of being unable to receive earned pension benefits while simultaneously being one of few workers not receiving pension contributions from their employer may contribute to worker dissatisfaction.

The monetary effects of not receiving wage or service credits may be substantial for a worker continuing in employment from age 65 to 70. For example, assume that a firm providing a defined benefit pension plan utilizes a formula in which benefits are determined by multiplying 1% of the final 5 years' average pay times the years of service. A worker with 30 years of service and a pay rate of $20,000 would receive an annual pension of $6,000 at age 65. If the worker receives wage and service pension accruals after age 65 and received moderate cost-of-living increases, his or her pension benefit may change substantially. By age 70, his new average final pay might be $25,000 multiplied by 35 years — an annual benefit of $8,750 for a 46% increase in retirement benefits. The increase is even greater for individuals with fewer years of service — the workers most likely to desire to continue working past age 65. Using the same formula, a worker with a final average pay of $20,000 and 15 years of service would receive an annual pension of $3,000. Pension credits for an additional 5 years work on a final average pay of $25,000 would provide a $5,000 year pension — an increase of 67% in retirement benefits. During this 5 year period the employer would, of course, gain the advantage provided by the use of the money which would have been paid out in pension benefits had the worker retired. Assuming that the worker is still a contributing, productive employee, the combination of investment return and a reduction in the number of years in retirement over which the pension benefits must be paid out, should ensure that the employer is not penalized by the continuing pension accruals.

These provisions have three distinct effects on the labor force participation of eligible workers beyond the normal retirement age. First, workers whose benefits are not adjusted actuarily lose value in their pensions at a rate of approximately 8 to 9% per year: this actuarial rate reflects the losses borne by workers in the asset value of their pensions. Second, that portion of the overall compensation package which relates to pension value is lost to the worker after the normal retirement age: this practice parallels a drop in earnings. Finally, continued work does not alter the value of the post-retirement income stream represented by pensions, an effect shown to be of particular interest to older workers.

In all, these practices constitute significant disincentives to continued employment among pensionable workers, though they represent significant sources of cost savings to employers. In spite of these potential savings, however, many employers are exceeding the minimum standards set by law by adjusting defined pension benefits in conformance with one or more of the adjustments identified above. Hewitt Associates found that 23% of firms responding to their survey adjust workers' benefits both for service and earnings changes realized after the normal retirement age and another 4.8% adjust benefits for only one or the other of these.[34] A second recent survey found that of those firms planning to offer accruals past the normal retirement age, 77% planned to adjust pensions for service accrued after the age of normal retirement, and that 71% intended to honor earnings changes during this phase of the career. Both surveys found that only approximately 50% of responding companies plan to offer no credits for service and earnings changes after the normal retirement age.

Other types of pension programs can be distinguished from defined benefit plans in that the plans are not designed to provide a stated level of benefits at retirement. These approaches to pension provision are discussed below.

Defined contribution plans are provided through the employer or other work-related entity, as are the defined benefit plans discussed above. Unlike defined benefit programs, however, benefits in defined contribution plans are determined by the amount of assets accumulated by a worker during the covered worklife: pension contributions are made periodically (typically annually) by the employer or may entail a combination of employee contributions with employer matching. The plan formula prescribes how much is to be contributed and how it is allocated to individual employee accounts. Under a defined contribution thrift or savings plan the contributions are based on a percentage of the employee's earnings matched in full or part by employer contributions. Under a defined contribution profit sharing plan the employer's contribution is based on annual profits and divided among employees according to their respective earnings. Unlike the defined benefit plan, the size of a defined contribution retirement account cannot be predicted in advance. The ultimate sum available upon retirement will depend on the size of contributions and the return on investments. Under defined contribution plans, the employee bears the risk of investments. Defined contribution plans are simpler to administer for employers since they pay an established amount each year and do not need to concern themselves with the future. Defined contribution plans are particularly attractive to newer and smaller firms or those with short-term workers.[35]

Deferred profit sharing plans are similar in many ways to the defined contribution plans described above. They may differ in that the amount of employer contributions to individual pensions are determined through the company's profitability, and typically by the proportion of covered payroll represented by the worker's earnings. Two types of profit sharing programs predominate. The first involves discretionary company contributions, where a gross sum identified by the company is divided among workers in accordance with relative salaries: the 1978 ADEA amendments will likely have little impact on the costs of these plans, since the amount contributed to the programs is determined by the company. The second type of profit sharing program is termed the "fixed formula" plan, where a fixed percentage of total payroll is contributed.

Thrift plans involve the employer's matching of employee contributions to the retirement fund. While the employee's own contribution is taken from taxed income, the employer's contribution and interest generated by both are not taxed until funds are disbursed. To the extent that older workers might well contribute more to pension plans, it has been suggested that the delay of mandatory retirement to age 70 would lead to higher company expenditures under thrift plans.

Individual Retirement Accounts (IRA's) are of relatively recent derivation, having been established as part of ERISA in 1974. Designed to permit the expansion of pensions' favored treatments under the tax codes, IRA's allow workers to save for retirement subject to an annual maximum of $2,000 for an individual or $2,250 for a couple. Neither the IRA deposit nor the interest accumulating to the account are taxed at the time they are earned, but rather at the time of dispersal. Generally maintained at commercial savings institutions, these funds generate relatively high (in the context of commercial interest rates) rates of return, subject to interest penalties for early withdrawal. Withdrawals without penalty may be undertaken between the ages of 59 1/2 and 70 1/2, and accumulated funds may be shielded from taxation through "rolling over," or their immediate deposit into an annuity or other protected savings or disbursal mechanism. The availability of IRA's may be attractive to older employees who are not covered by pension accruals past their normal retirement age or employees who begin part-time work after retirement. However, the upper age limit of seventy may provide constraints on the continued utilization of IRA's by older persons. The requirement that withdrawals begin at age 70 1/2 may have adverse effect on workers employed beyond this age.

Keough plans are named for the senator who pushed for their initial introduction. Keough plans allow the self-employed to generate retirement funds through tax deductible contributions of up to an annual maximum of $15,000 into accounts at financial institutions. Keough legislation requires similar contributions for other employees, and this requirement is credited with leading to a lessened rate of expansion in Keough account openings since IRA's, which bear no such requirement, were introduced.

Simplified Employee Pensions (SEP's) are a relatively new addition to the array of pension mechanisms available to employers, having been introduced as part of the 1978 Revenue Act. SEP's allow employer contribution to IRA's of as high as $15,000 though tests of discrimination are in some cases more restrictive than are applied to other types of plans. SEP's tend to favor short-term employees to a greater extent than do other types of pension programs, a characteristic possibly to the detriment of employers seeking to reward long-term employees. Like IRA's, however, SEP's offer low administrative costs, reduced fiduciary liability, and pension portability.

General Disincentives to Work Among Pensions

While disincentives to work specific to primary pension plans were discussed earlier, there remains a significant disincentive to continued employment, a common requirement of company sponsored pension programs. Virtually all defined benefit, defined contribution, profit sharing, and thrift plans require the worker to leave the employ of the pension-providing organization before pension benefits are payable. This is an important requirement, for it introduces a potential discontinuity in the older worker's career: to leave established employment and continue working requires the individual to find other work. Real or perceived age discrimination, in addition to the common problems in obtaining new employment, may discourage older workers from seeking new employment. Once unemployed, older workers take longer to find employment and are more likely to find work of lesser status and pay than are younger job seekers. There is good reason to expect that the need to find re-employment will in and of itself, as well as in conjunction with the availability of pension income, influence many to leave the labor force.

Prevalent practices associated with pensions tend to influence workers away from continued employment once they qualify for benefits. The lack of pension benefit accruals, the inability to receive pension benefits while continuing to work for the same employer, and other factors encourage workers to retire. Compounding these influences prevalent in private pension plans are those which accompany the most broadly available single source of retirement income in the country, the social security programs. This topic constitutes the focus of the section which follows.

Social Security

Social Security legislation grew out of the depression era. Passed into law as the Old Age Insurance program (OAI) in 1935, the law was amended to add survivors coverage in 1939, and disability insurance in 1956. Throughout its history, the Social Security Administration has expanded continually in terms both of coverages offered and workers covered. As suggested above, survivors and disability benefits were incorporated early in the program's development. A later addition involved health insurance a product of the 1965 passage of Medicare legislation. The addition of the Supplemental Security Income (SSI) program to the Social Security Administration's administrative auspice rounded out the administration's present offerings. The constant growth of the programs is reflected in the number of workers covered under social security. By 1979 social security covered 90% of the labor force, and was paying benefits to 94% of all retired households.[36]

Though employing trust funds of modest size, all social security programs except Medicare and SSI are essentially funded on a "pay-as-you-go" basis in which current revenues are employed in meeting current liabilities. This financing mechanism is in large part responsible for short- and long-term concerns over the Administration's ability to meet its obligations under the existing financing scheme. As the proportion of the population of retired beneficiaries grows relative to the working population which funds the programs, the incidence of taxation needed to meet liabilities must also expand. Towers, Perrin, Forster and Crosby,[37] for example, have predicted that the beneficiary-to-worker ratio will increase from approximately 1:3 in 1978 to a level of about 1:2 in the year 2030, and that revenues will grow from 8.2% of GNP in 1977 to as high as 14% of GNP by 1990.

Further exacerbating potential funding problems for the Social Security Administration are the counter-cyclical tendencies of its programs. Rates of retirement, for example, tend to escalate in times of high unemployment causing total benefits to grow. At the same time, rising unemployment diminishes the program's revenues: Boskin has estimated that each 1/2% drop in GNP growth adds approximately $100 billion to the Social Security Administration's deficit.

Disincentives to Work

In this context, one means of alleviating the financial pressures on social security lies in the lengthening of the worklife, and the equivalent shortening of retirement: the former extends the period of individual's contributions, while the latter reduces liabilities. It is generally conceded, however, that the Old Age and Survivors programs offer a number of disincentives to labor force participation extended beyond the age of 65, and some would suggest that these disincentives are felt as early as age 62. The Congressional Research Service, for example, identifies three elements of the social security programs which encourage retirement. The first and most fundamental is the existence of the benefit itself. Alternative sources of income other than work allow persons to maintain income flows into the future while retiring from the labor force. The other two disincentives to work are integral parts of current program which could be changed by future legislation. The following sections describe the major disincentives to work which are a product of the social security system.

Social Security Benefit

Philip L. Rones notes that, "the most significant factor in (the decline in labor force participation rates among men over 60) is the growing

financial ability of older men to retire early.''[38] As benefits are tied
to the absence of earnings above $6,000 per year (for those aged
65 to 71), the existence of benefits may be characterized as an opportunity cost associated with work. The degree to which this opportunity cost is a prime determinant in the decision to work or retire is
likely to be directly related to the amount of earned after-tax income
available to the individual if he or she continued to work versus the
tax free, indexed benefits available under social security. The pro-
gressivity of the social security program is a factor in this determination, as replacement rates (the relationship between retirement benefits and the pre-retirement earnings needed to generate them) are
higher at lower income levels than those provided for retirees who had
higher incomes. As such, one would anticipate that the existence of
the benefit as a sole source of labor force withdrawal would be a
more powerful influence among workers in the lower income ranges.

Early and Delayed Retirement Adjustments. The computation of
basic benefits under social security, as with many private pensions,
assumes retirement at age 65. Departures from this practice allow
retirement as early as age 62, and delayed retirement indefinitely.
Early retirement is accompanied by benefit reductions which closely
correspond to actuarial rates of reduction and therefore can be considered largely age-neutral as a retirement incentive. The delayed retirement credit, however, is calculated at the rate of only 1% per
year. This credit falls far short of the actuarially derived adjustment
which would be necessary to sustain the value of total benefits to
the worker. Current mortality tables reflect that this figure would
be approximately 8 to 9% per year between the ages of 65 and 72.[39]
The difference between the actuarially derived figure and the 1% adjustment currently employed means that the value of total benefits
to be received by the individual is decreased by 7 to 8% for each
year the worker refrains from claiming social security benefits. This
income is lost to the individual and never recovered. The Congressional
Research Service correctly concludes that the prevailing structure of
adjustments discourages labor force participation among older workers, and recommends changes which could alter the existing program.[40] The first change involves altering the basis on which reductions in benefits accompanying early retirement are determined. By

shifting the reductions from the current actuarial basis to the cost of capital, effective reduction rates would be increased by approximately 50%, or from 20% to 30% for those retiring at age 62. This recommendation poses a net disincentive to early retirement, and, not incidentally, a net saving to the Social Security Administration. The second recommendation would increase the delayed retirement credit to actuarial levels of 8 to 9%. This would remove the disincentive to work currently posed by the delayed retirement credit. While it would not save costs it would likely expand revenues as more older workers remain on the job.

The Retirement Test. The retirement test is an administratively straight-forward way to ensure that individuals otherwise eligible for benefits also qualify by having withdrawn from the labor force. A 1982 example illustrates how it works: for each $2 earned above $6,000 by individuals aged 65 to 72 ($4,400 by those under 65) a $1 reduction in social security benefits is imposed until benefits are totally eliminated. The retirement test has the effect of halving the financial benefits derived through employment for those with incomes exceeding relevant threshold levels. In this sense, the test is frequently likened to a 50% tax on the earnings of affected workers. The effects of the retirement test are widespread and considerable. One estimate numbers those actually losing benefits through this mechanism in 1975 at approximately 1.7 million people, and this estimate does not include persons who refrained from working altogether because of the retirement test or those who structured their work-time so as not to exceed the maximum unpenalized earnings level set by the retirement test.[41] If the computations were based on the years since 1975, greater numbers of individuals would have been affected. Few would argue that the retirement test is the strongest disincentive to work associated with the social security programs. In other research, the authors have found that older workers and employers frequently cite the retirement test as one of the primary influences discouraging older workers from continuing in the labor force. This observation is consistent with labor force figures which indicate that fully 28% of those age 65 who work do so on a part-time basis.[42]

The effects on earnings of the retirement test are exacerbated by the tax codes. The earnings which lead to the displacement of social security benefits are taxable as income, while the displaced benefits themselves are not. As a result, net contributions to disposable income of earnings are actually less than even the 50% reduction imposed by the retirement test would imply. Addressing *only* the retirement test and federal income taxation, Burkhauser estimates that the median worker in 1980 would realize a 75% rate of taxation on earnings.[43] In reality, most workers would also have to pay additional state income taxes and the employee share of the social security payroll tax out of their employment earnings. When these taxes are added to the usual costs of employment such as commuting expenses, clothes and meals, it is surprising that any eligible beneficiaries choose to earn more than the retirement test threshold. The retirement test has been the subject of considerable debate for many years. Recently, it has been defended primarily in terms of the costs associated with its removal. One such defense estimates that removal of the test would generate costs of $2.16 billion annually, of which approximately $679 would be offset by increases in revenues derived through employment.[44] The Congressional Research Service, in a similar analysis, generates estimates of total costs in the area of $7 billion annually.[45] Of these, approximately $2 billion would accrue from workers over 65, and approximately $5.6 billion would involve workers under 65. In large measure, however, the findings of these analyses are limited by the samples used in the studies and the analytical strategies incorporated in their design. The Gordon and Schoenplein analysis, for example, is based only on those who actually lost benefits in the targeted year. It is reasonable to anticipate that a different approach to the identification and measurement of impacts would yield different results. Those whose work involvements yield less earnings than needed to trigger the retirement test could expand earnings, for example, without forcing greater expenditures by the Social Security Administration, and would yield greater revenues through heightened taxes on earnings. Similarly, those whose withdrawal from the labor force is in part occasioned by the retirement test could return without affecting the social security administration's disbursements, while expanding on the payroll tax base of the agency's programs. Both of these sources of change would temper the net costs estimated through the studies typically undertaken to date, and merit further exploration.

Without question the current social security program operates to reduce work incentives and encourage retirement. Given the fiscal problems of the social security system and the demographic changes which are likely to result in labor supply shortages, the system as it presently operates should be modified. Burkhauser summarizes his views on social security as follows: "Changes are not necessary because the system failed, it didn't, but because it continues to apply cures developed for past social ills to a country suffering from different social ailments."[46]

In this context, the major challenge facing policymakers in adapting the social security programs to current and future conditions lies in adopting realistic assessments of the programs' provisions on the behaviors of covered and pensioned populations, and to develop alternative provisions where necessary in order to alter incentives and disincentives not in keeping with current national priorities.

Impacts on the Paycheck

The discussion which has preceded in this chapter provides a relatively complete description of the impacts of age and, in particular, retirement eligibility on the effective remuneration of workers. The test gives little indication, however, of how all of these forces combine to affect the value of the pay package. As reflected in Table 4-1, the impacts can be severe. Table entries demonstrate the impact of each age-related disincentive on the value of the remunerative package received by workers in each of four selected situations. Starting with a total remunerative scheme valued at 140% of nominal wage, including fringe benefits equal to 40% of payroll, the table suggests that as much as 104% of nominal earnings can be lost to the worker who continues in employment in lieu of retirement.

Factors described earlier are classified in terms of two broad classes of costs: Direct Costs and Opportunity Costs.

Direct Costs are those which directly reduce the worker's total income while working, but which would not be borne in retirement. The social security retirement test, for example, reduces the benefit of recipients by 50% in the relevant earnings ranges, an expense clearly not incurred in retirement. Social security contributions, leveled only on earnings, similarly affect the worker. Because social security benefits are not taxed, taxes falling on workers tend to be higher than those levied against retirees: including federal, state, and local income taxes, the 10% cited in the table is likely to be conservative in most

Table 4-1. Decrements to remunerative value among retirable workers as a percent of nominal earning by social security status and age. (Monetary Earnings = 100, Fringe Benefits = 40, Total Package = 140.)

| | SOCIAL SECURITY STATUS | | | |
| | COLLECTING BENEFITS | | DELAYING BENEFITS | |
CLASS OF DECREMENT	AGE 62	AGE 65	AGE 62	AGE 65
Direct Costs				
Social Security Retirement Test[1]	50	50	0	0
Social Security Withholding Taxes[2]	13[3]	13[3]	13[3]	13[3]
Income Taxes	10	10	10	10
Pension Contributions	0	6	0	6
Life Insurance	0	0	0	0
Health Insurance	0	0	0	0
Disability Insurance	0	0	0	0
Opportunity Costs				
Pension Benefits (in lieu of actuarial adjustments)[4]	0	25	0	25
Social Security Benefits (including Delayed Retirement Credit)[5]	0	0	0	35
Total Decrements	73	104	23	79
Net Value of Remunerative Package (as percent of nominal earnings)	67	36	117	61

NOTES

[1] In 1982, affects earnings over $4400 for workers age 62–64, $6000 for workers age 65–71. Workers over age 72 are not affected by the Social Security Retirement Test.
[2] Affects first $32,400 of earnings in 1982.
[3] Actual decrement is 13.4%.
[4] Assuming 25% replacement rate, Normal Retirement Age of 65, actuarial adjustments before age 65, and no adjustments after age 65.
[5] Assuming 40% replacement rate at age 65. Adjustments for retirement between ages 62 and 65 are subject to reductions of 6 2/3% per year, while retirement after age 65 generates a delayed retirement credit of 1% per year.

cases. Finally, because pension contributions are not required after the normal retirement age, they too are lost to the worker. As legislated by ADEA, the values represented by life, health, and disability insurance coverages remain intact.

Opportunity Costs are income sources which are foregone through continued work: while not deducted from the pay check, their availability reduces the advantages associated with work. For those whose pension benefits are not actuarily adjusted to reflect work after the normal retirement age, any benefits foregone through work after that age are lost to the worker. Similarly, the low rates of adjustment associated with social security benefits after the age of 65 can generate a loss in value to the worker of as much as 32% of nominal wage.

Overall, workers qualifying for a retirement income program cannot avoid losses in the value of their pay packages. As suggested in Table 4-1, the size of the loss incurred is a reflection of the worker's age and status with respect to social security benefits, as well as a host of other factors. Together, these can reduce the monetary incentives associated with continued employment dramatically. In this context, it is not surprising that so few people over the age of 65 continue on the job: more startling is the fact that fully 20% continue in the labor market in spite of these influences.

CONCLUSION

Older workers could well be one of the few groups in the nation's population who are required to lose income in order to work. This chapter has addressed a number of characteristics associated with present remunerative practices which tend to influence older workers away from employment and into retirement. Prevalent practises which affect the retirement decisions of older workers arise from government retirement income programs and tax policies as well as the monetary and non-monetary compensation policies of individual employers. The effects of a number of these policies are highlighted below:

- Earned income is generally subject to immediate taxation while social security income is not. The different tax treatment of the two potential income sources weakens the attraction of work for eligible individuals.

- The retirement test of the social security program results in substantial penalties for beneficiaries who earn more than a minimal threshold level of income. The 50% reduction in benefits is a significant disincentive to work.
- If pensions are not actuarially adjusted after the normal retirement age, the worker bears the hidden cost of lost pension benefits. This is a net loss of 8 to 9% a year in the undiscounted value of the pension.
- In the absence of actuarial adjustments to social security benefits, the worker bears the hidden cost of lost social security benefits. This is a net cost of 8 to 9% a year for workers over age 65.
- In the absence of pension credits for wage and/or service after the normal retirement age, the worker loses that portion of the pay package which previously went to pension contributions.
- If the worker is compulsorily enrolled in fringe benefit programs which provide benefits of little value to the worker, the value derived through these elements of a pay package is diminished.
- If the worker must sustain costs associated with work but not with retirement, these expenses reduce the value of earnings.
- If workers are unable to receive their pension benefits while continuing to work for the same employer, the value of continued earnings is diminished.

In short, continued work may not be an economically viable alternative for most American workers eligible for retirement income programs. Early retirement, encouraged by actuarial reductions in social security programs and frequently by less than actuarial reductions in private pension programs, may well represent a more attractive and financially favorable alternative.

The complex set of policies which shape the morass of incentives and disincentives will not be simple to change. ERISA restricts pension provisions. ADEA extends many but not all privileges of employment to older workers. IRS codes govern taxation policies which differentially affect income sources. Employer policies may reflect many different orientations due to operational and market-related factors.

The effectiveness of changing any one component in this system will depend on the interrelation between the new system and the many other related systems.

The successful implementation of programs which encourage older individuals to stay on the job must also involve the "dovetailing" of employment and remunerative policies. The importance of this observation cannot be overstated. The complex network of personal preferences and institutional forces surrounding retirement requires that effective programs or policies address the job itself, current income, and eventual retirement income. Changing one factor, such as the hours of work, may not be effective if changes in the pay package continue to penalize continued work. Employers who develop remunerative policies which allow older individuals employment options may benefit through increased flexibility in their human resource plans and a wider pool of potential workers.

FOOTNOTES

1. *Webster's Third New International Dictionary of the English Language, Unabridged,* Springfield, Massachusetts: G and C Merriam Company, 1967.
2. Malcolm H. Morrison. "The Future of Flexible Retirement," *College and University Personnel Association Journal,* Winter 1978.
3. Raymond A. Katzell and Daniel Yankelovich. *Work, Productivity and Job Satisfaction: An Evaluation of Policy-Related Research.* New York: Harcourt, Brace and Javanovich, Inc., 1975.
4. J. Brad Chapman and Robert Otterman. "Employee Preferences for Various Compensation and Fringe Benefit Options," in William F. Glueck (ed.), *Personnel: A Book of Readings.* Dallas: Business Publications, Inc., 1979.
5. Ibid.
6. Stanley M. Nealey and S. G. Goodale. "Workers Preferences Among Time-Off Benefits and Pay," *Journal of Applied Psychology,* August 1967.
7. Robert V. Goode. "Complications at the Cafeteria Checkout Line," *Personnel,* November–December 1974.
8. William V. Machaver. "Employee Benefits: Promises and Realities," in David A. Weeks (ed.) *Rethinking Employee Benefits Assumptions.* New York: The Conference Board, Inc., 1978.
9. Susan Koralik. "Implications of Government Policy-Making in Employee Compensation and Benefits," in David A. Weeks (ed.), *Rethinking Employee Benefits Assumptions.* New York: The Conference Board, 1978.
10. Philip L. Rones. "Older Men – The Choice Between Work and Retirement," *Monthly Labor Review,* November 1978.

11. Richard Burkhauser. Written Testimony to the Subcommittee on Oversight of the Committee on Ways and Means, U.S. House of Representatives, September 10, 1980.
12. Robert Clark. *Adjusting Hours to Increase Jobs,* Special Report #15, A Special Report of the National Commission for Manpower Policy, September 1977.
13. Richard Barfield and James Morgan. *Early Retirement: The Decision and the Experience.* Ann Arbor: University of Michigan, 1969.
14. Herbert S. Parnes (ed.). *Work and Retirement: A Longitudinal Study of Men.* Cambridge, Massachusetts: MIT Press, 1981.
15. Irwin Sober. *Employment: Background and Issues.* Washington, D.C.: White House Conference on Aging, March 1971.
16. James H. Schulz. *The Economics of Aging.* Belmont, California: Wadsworth Publishing Company, Second Edition, 1980.
17. Juanita M. Kreps. *Lifetime Allocation of Work and Income.* Durham, N.C.: Duke University Press, 1971.
18. Dorothy Fleisher McConnel, Carolyn E. Usher, and Barbara Hale Kaplan. *Alternative Work Options for Older Workers,* Andrus Gerontology Center, University of Southern California, 1980.
19. Lois A. Copperman and Fred D. Keast. "In the Wake of ADEA," final report for the President's Commission on Pension Policy, Portland, Oregon: Institute on Aging, Portland State University, February 1980.
20. Ibid.
21. Machaver, op. cit.
22. Machaver, op. cit.
23. Chapman and Otterman, op. cit.
24. Goode, op. cit.
25. Nealey and Goodale, op. cit.
26. Johnson and Higgins. *1979 Study of American Attitudes Toward Pensions and Retirement,* conducted by Harris Associates, New York: Johnson and Higgins, 1979.
27. Edward E. Lawler, III. "New Approaches to Pay: Innovations that Work," *Personnel,* September–October 1956.
28. Hewitt Associates. *Benefit Issues Regarding the Age Discrimination in Employment Act,* Compensation Exchange, Hewitt Associates, January 1980.
29. Goode, op. cit.
30. Lawler, op. cit.
31. Koralik, op. cit.
32. Hewitt Associates, op. cit.
33. Employee Benefit Research Institute (EBRI). *Defined Benefit and Defined Contribution Plans: Understanding the Differences.* Washington, D.C.: EBRI, Pamphlet N. 110–16, 1981.
34. Hewitt Associates, op. cit.
35. Employee Benefit Research Institute, op. cit.
36. Meier and Ditmar, op. cit.

37. Towers, Perrin, Forster and Crosby. *Pensions, Social Security Benefits: Levels, Costs and Issues.* Washington, D.C.: Business Roundtable, 1979.
38. Rones, op. cit.
39. Congressional Research Service. "Background Material on Work, Retirement and Social Security," Washington, D.C.: U.S. Government Printing Office, 1980.
40. Ibid.
41. Ibid.
42. Rones, op. cit.
43. Burkhauser, op. cit.
44. Josephine A. Gordon and Robert N. Schoeplein. "The Impact from Elimination of the Retirement Test," *Social Security Bulletin,* September 1979.
45. Congressional Research Service, op. cit.
46. Burkhauser, op. cit.

5
Models for Change:
Innovative Employer Policies

INTRODUCTION

Older workers and the complex issues surrounding retirement decisions will be the central manpower concerns of the next decade. Business and government leaders are as unprepared to cope with these
issues now as they were to confront the questions of minority employment in the 60s and women's issues in the 1970s. Yet during the
transitional period in which policies are adjusted to discourage retirement, considerable information on alternatives to present policies will
be required. To be effective new private and public policies must be
based on a clear statement of priorities, as well as a sound understanding of the preferences of older workers and the policies which affect
their retirement decisions. Since future policies will alter the retirement plans and behavior of millions of individuals, the policies must be
carefully developed and phased in gradually in an equitable manner.

While a well considered and thoughtfully drafted plan to alter
existing retirement patterns would include both contributions from
government and from the private sector, no such plan appears to be
forthcoming. A number of companies, however, have independently
developed programs which are effective in retaining older workers in
the labor force. The major thrust of this chapter is to identify common characteristics of these programs and to present a number of
examples of what can be — and have been — done.

As was suggested earlier, labor force participation rates of males
aged 45 to 64 have declined steadily during this century. Reversing
the trend toward early retirement will require significant political,
social and economic changes. The strong trend toward early retirement suggests that given an adequate income in retirement and lacking strong incentives to remain in employment, most older workers
prefer to withdraw from the labor force. Present information suggests

that policies which simply provide the opportunity for older workers to continue on the job will fail to result in significant changes in retirement patterns. Successful attempts to change or reverse the trend toward early retirement will require a sound base of knowledge concerning the incentives and disincentives to retirement, as well as the development of new human resource policies by individual employers which encourage the utilization of older workers.

Nationally, past experience as well as common sense suggest that retirement patterns are sensitive to change in retirement policies. There is little doubt that the trend toward early retirement could be quickly reversed by reducing or eliminating social security and private pension plan benefits for persons who retire prior to age 65. However, to ensure a smooth and fair transition in retirement ages with minimum adverse impacts, alterations in retirement benefits must be made over time. Present retirement benefits have formed an integral part in the calculations of older employees approaching retirement and the human resource plans and capabilities of employers. An abrupt shift in retirement benefit policies would cause dislocation and undesirable consequences for both individuals and organizations. To affect desirable changes in retirement patterns, we need to know more about the retirement and employment decisions of individuals, how employer policies and government policies affect the labor force participation rates of older individuals, and how employer policies, government policies and individuals' retirement and employment decisions interact with one another.

SOURCES OF VARIATION IN OLDER WORKER PROGRAMS

Individual employers are only now beginning to reexamine the policies which affect older workers and, more proactively, to develop policies which favorably influence their firms while also addressing the needs of older workers. A considerable variation is apparent among the various "older worker" policies and programs which are being developed. In general, this variation can be traced to three broad sources: the motivations which moved employers to implement their programs, the roles within the employing organizations identified as appropriate for targeted older workers, and the planning and decisionmaking processes which led to program development and implementation. Each of these points bears individual attention.

The motivations which compel organizations to develop innovative policies for older workers are many and varied; they include current labor supply shortages, projected future manpower shortages, desires to meet the employment needs of their older workers, pension funding problems, and a host of other factors. Despite increasing interest in older workers and retirement issues, the vast majority of employers continue to employ personnel policies which have been developed to accommodate the very young labor markets of the past two decades. Few companies have planned or projected for their human resource needs on more than a short run basis. Consequently, only a small minority of employers have developed an active interest in planning and adopting new programs which will retain or attract older workers. A 1981 survey of large employers by William Mercer, Incorporated found that many employers believe that inflation and other factors will make people postpone retirement. In the 1990s the companies will have a larger proportion of older individuals. Almost one in four of the employer respondents are changing their human resource planning to reflect the decline in size of the younger labor pool and an additional third expect to do such planning within 5 years.[1]

Those firms which have adopted or considered new policies and programs broadly reflect one or more of the following characteristics.

- Labor supply shortages in particular skills or occupations.
- Labor supply shortages in their geographical areas.
- Management attitudes which dictate a humane posture toward all employees, and consideration of workers as assets.
- Legislative mandates to develop alternative work options.
- Large size.
- The provision of pensions and fringe benefits.
- Non-union.
- Variation in the need for workers due to seasonal, cyclical or recurrent fluctuations in the demand for or supply of labor.

Firms demonstrating one or more of these characteristics are more likely than other companies to have undertaken the tasks of considering and adopting personnel and remunerative practices designed to attract or retain older workers. Many high technology aerospace companies located in living areas with high housing costs and critical labor shortages, for example, have introduced innovative programs oriented to older workers. Yet the factors influencing employers to develop such programs necessarily reflect the operational contexts within which the firms operate. As a result, employers with innovative programs for older workers reflect considerable variation in motivations.

Just as the motivations for implementing programs such as these are subject to considerable variation between employers, so are the programs themselves. An increasing number of personnel professionals are familiar with the fact that different combinations of personnel and remunerative policies are capable of producing quite distinct behaviors among employees of different types. As a result, desired ends can be choreographed to an extent through the selective application of different employment and remunerative practices. This general rule of personnel administration applies to older workers just as it does to other components of the labor force.

For this reason, and because companies with innovative programs for older workers tend to be reacting to different motivating conditions, employers' programs designed to appeal to older workers vary considerably. One useful basis upon which to classify these programs focuses upon the role of affected workers in the organization. More specifically, programs designed to promote older workers' employment as members of the organization's primary labor force generally differ in important ways from those which address older workers as members of the secondary labor force.

The primary labor force in this context is that component of the employer's work force which is comprised of management, production workers, and other employees engaged in tasks which are necessary to the production and administration of the firm. The primary labor force is that group which is traditionally understood to comprise the company's core group of workers. Primary workers are often also distinguishable from members of the secondary labor force in that they are accorded fringe benefits as a component in the remunerative package while secondary workers typically are not. Primary jobs are characterized by security and permanence of employment. Additionally, primary jobs generally offer better wages, upward mobility and full benefits. All employers have a primary labor force.

The secondary labor force is comprised broadly of everyone else. These workers tend to be temporary or short term. They may be

DIFFERENTIATING CHARACTERISTIC	PRIMARY LABOR FORCE	SECONDARY LABOR FORCE
Expected Duration of Employment	Permanent	Temporary
Typical Remunerative Package	Monetary and Fringes	Monetary Only
Susceptability to Labor Force Contraction	Low	High
Stability of Task Assignment	High	Low
Promotional Opportunities	High	Low

Figure 5-1. Prevalent characteristics — primary and secondary labor forces.

hired to work on particular projects or tasks and their employment may end once the task or project is completed. As suggested above, pay packages extended to an employer's secondary labor force tend to include few if any fringe benefits. Secondary jobs are generally characterized by relatively low wages, little job security, limited upward mobility and high turnover. Many firms have no secondary labor force.

Figure 5-1 summarizes a number of important characteristics which frequently differentiate primary and secondary labor forces.

As might be anticipated from the preceding discussion, the employment offerings extended to older workers recruited as primary workers are likely to differ markedly from those developed for members of a secondary labor force. In addressing the primary labor force through older workers, the challenge facing the employer is to lure people away from retirement, whether they are retired already or merely contemplating it: the task lies in making the job worth the effort. Monetary remuneration is an important factor, but, as was noted in earlier discussion, a number of factors tend to diminish the value of earnings for many retirable workers. Since much of the value represented in many pay packages is reflected in the fringe benefits extended to members of the primary labor force, these also merit attention. To the extent that nonmonetary benefits extended to active employees paralleled those included in the retirement package, they exert less influence to continue working.

Characteristics of the job itself may also require modification. As suggested earlier, reductions in stress and expanded temporal flexibility may lessen the apparent attraction of retirement among workers otherwise well suited for continued employment. In sum, efforts expended in retaining or attracting many older workers to the primary labor force entail the development of complete pay and work packages which are worthwhile and motivate this specific group of employees.

The development of programs or policies offering secondary jobs is substantially different. First, since fringe benefits are typically not offered to this type of employee, potential duplications represent no problem. Second, since potential durations of employment are likely to be shorter than those encountered in the primary labor force, the impediments to employment posed by the retirement test and by differential tax treatments tend to be of less importance. Similarly, since pension benefits are not necessarily extended to participants in the secondary labor force by the employing firm, interruption or delay of retirement benefits are not factors in the workers' employment decision. The older worker may be securing pension benefits and the income from the job is considered as supplemental. These factors tend to enhance the value of the pay package associated with retired or retirable workers in the secondary labor force and, where fringe benefits have been extended as part of these individuals' retirement packages, may even effectively subsidize their employment.

Utilizing older workers as a source of supply for a secondary labor force is a relatively new and growing practice. The pool of older individuals interested in employment is unique in that many of its members would traditionally be characterized as primary workers – skilled, experienced individuals who have in many cases had long tenure in their jobs. Traditionally, secondary jobs with low wages, few promotional opportunities and little job security have not appealed to this class of worker. Yet, for many older pensioned workers these criteria alone may not necessarily make secondary jobs unattractive. The desire for leisure time and the presence of another income source – i.e., pensions – may alter their assessment of a job's suitability. Older workers are generally not setting out on a new long-term career and consequently may have less interest in eventual promotional opportunities than would otherwise be the case. Given flexible hours, secondary jobs may, in fact, appeal to older individuals.

This potential labor pool offers great opportunities to employers. Projects or tasks which traditionally required skills available only among the primary work force could be performed by many older workers. Such projects could be structured in a fashion which would attract skilled, experienced older individuals without incurring the long-term costs associated with primary jobs.

Since many older workers already have basic income derived from pension, social security payments, and savings, they may move in and out of the labor force with relatively less hardship than younger heads of household whose sole incomes are derived from employment. Many older workers who have held positions in the primary work force may enter the secondary labor force on retirement. In essence, firms which develop tasks are utilizing the older secondary labor force. The skills and experience of these older workers make them attractive employees. Firms employing them on a short-term or temporary basis are able to take advantage of the personnel flexibility which such a labor force offers. In developing policies and programs employers should carefully consider the type of labor force they wish to attract or retain and tailor their personnel and remunerative packages to the needs of this group.

In all, then, in addition to the variation evident in employers' motivations for implementing programs for older workers, additional differences are introduced through the roles perceived for targeted workers in the employing organization. These differentiating factors, however, are further compounded by the nature of the planning and decisionmaking processes which lead to the implementation of such a plan. Considerable room is available for experimentation in developing specific programs or policies which meet both the needs of the employer and the preferences of older workers. Such programs may be structured in many different ways. The descriptions of employer programs in the following discussion should provide food for thought.

While much of the preceding discussion has addressed the development of innovative programs targeted at older workers as a tightly rational process, it is apparent that in most cases other approaches to program development were also operating.

The models presented in this book demonstrate the nature of the decision-making processes which have resulted in the adoption of progressive employment practices. In most cases the policies were developed in an ad hoc manner rather than as a result of carefully considered, rationalized institutional planning. Few companies have initiated innovative older worker programs as the result of forecasts of their future labor supply requirements and the labor supply likely to be available to the firm in the near or distant future. Instead policies have been adopted as a result of individual employee requests, needs identified in employee surveys conducted for other purposes, the "bright ideas" of individual managers, and other relatively casual factors. Carefully designed and crafted human resource plans which have identified a need for older workers and developed mechanisms for attracting or retaining them are few and far between.

Once adopted, innovative programs are rarely monitored to determine their costs and benefits. The costs of the programs are generally not calculated specifically and the benefits of the program are not known. Little or no attempt is made to examine participation or non-participation in particular programs to determine their impact. Clearly stated goals and objectives are uncommon. Follow-up evaluations and monitoring the success of the program in meeting goals are generally not performed by employers. Programs are offered, employees participate or don't participate, and the impacts of the programs are unknown. Most progressive employer policies have also been in effect for a relatively short period of time and managers have little long-term experience with the programs on which to base evaluations. Few employees have actually participated in a number of the more far-reaching programs and thus it is presently difficult to judge their success.

The costs of implementation, adoption and administration of most new programs are absorbed in general budgets and the figures on the specific program related costs are difficult or impossible to obtain from existing data. Generally, the return on investment from the programs is not known and the actual amount of investment in particular programs is not calculated. Many employers adopt policies intended to affect older workers without careful consideration of the integration of remunerative policies with personnel policies. The existing constraints of pension and benefit policies may be accepted as "givens" and policies which require alterations in pension policies, for example, are unlikely to be attempted. New programs which may be adopted without requiring revisions in existing policies are more likely to be considered or adopted. Policies are often developed without obtaining system-wide information on employee preferences for alternative policies. The manager of one large organization, which offers a number of programs which allow older workers to choose among a number of options, stated that the organization has no idea whether the programs have benefited the firm or the individual worker. No attempts to evaluate the costs and benefits of the program have been attempted. The programs were adopted to fit the employer's philosophy which emphasizes the development of the maximum potential of each individual worker. In brief, the consideration, adoption and implementation of employer policies and programs intended to attract or retain older workers is not generally a carefully considered, rationalized process with clearly identified costs and benefits derived from the programs. A minority of individual employers are currently experimenting with programs which are generally developed in an ad hoc manner to meet a vaguely identified and perhaps low priority need of the employer and/or its older workers.

In the pages which follow, a number of firms' programs are described. Representative of a range of industries and requirements, these companies provide general models of programs which might be adopted by other employers.

EMPLOYER PROGRAMS*

Since older workers and the jobs they occupy are necessarily diverse, the programs developed to attract or retain these members of the labor force are structured in many different ways. Basically, employers wishing to retain older workers in their full-time current position presently offer traditional job-related incentives to such individuals. The availability of pension benefit accruals past the normal retirement age and perhaps flexitime hours are the primary progressive incentives currently available to retain full-time permanent workers.

The innovative programs described in the remainder of this chapter provide variations in hours and benefits to allow older workers opportunities for increased leisure while continuing in employment. Within this general framework employers have developed programs ranging from temporary "on call" arrangements for low skilled annuitants to carefully negotiated phased retirement programs which are fully

---

*All employer and pension plan names used in this section are pseudonyms employed to protect the anonymity of the organizations described.

integrated with pension benefits. Programs which could be easily adapted or modified by other employers were selected for inclusion in this section. The following discussion, then, presents innovative employer policies and programs which have been developed to retain or attract older workers and which appear to be reasonably applicable to a range of employment situations.

It should be noted that many of the programs described in the following section are offering older workers employment in "secondary"-type jobs. The programs presented in this section reflect the type of programs presently being developed and offered by employers — as such they represent the initial responses of firms which are just beginning to focus on older worker issues. Hopefully, more innovative programs offering primary type jobs will be developed in the future so that older individuals will have a full range of available options.

Phased Retirement: Machines, Inc.

A large mid-western manufacturer of machinery has recently adopted a carefully developed program to retain their older workers. In 1977 the company initiated a study of their business projections as well as the demographic factors affecting their labor supply. Results of the study indicated that new college graduates were projected to fall between 6 and 8% below the levels of the late seventies. At the same time business projections for the eighties indicated the need for approximately 8% more new college graduates than currently hired. The combined projections indicated a shortfall between company needs and labor force supply of approximately 15%. The projections stimulated management to consider innovative sources of labor supply on a long term basis.

In searching for a solution to the projected labor supply problems, management examined the loss of skills to the company which occurs as a result of the early retirement of many of their older employees. Generally employees retire from the company at approximately age 60. To retain their older workers and to provide incentives to them for continued employment, the firm developed a carefully conceived partial retirement program which is described below.

Although the company has employed few part-time workers in the past, management recognized that the common limitations of temporary or casual part-time workers were eliminated if the part-time labor force was drawn from their own experienced older labor force. Consequently, they developed a particularly innovative new program in which almost all jobs are considered potentially adaptable to part-time employment including production supervisors, computer programmers, engineers, marketing specialists and production line workers. Under the new program two supervisors may share jobs. Persons with technical skills would be allowed to put all their time into one project rather than being assigned to two or three projects. In the case of jobs which are not adaptable to part-time employment, the employee and the employer would develop a mutual agreement on demotion.

Basically, the program of partial retirement is open to persons with 30 years of service credit or persons age 60 and over with 10 years of service credit. The eligible employee and the employer enter into a binding work agreement of one year's duration in which an assigned work schedule is specified and agreed upon. The work schedule could include part-day full week schedules; full-day, part week schedules; and other variations — provided that the employee works some period in each month. A participant may not, for example, work 3 months and then take off 3 months. The participant's remuneration is based on a pro-rated ratio of time not worked and time worked. Employees must work a minimum of 20% time and up to a maximum of 80% time. If an employee chooses to work 60% time, he or she will receive 60% of his or her full-time salary and 40% of his or her pension benefit. At the end of the 1 year period the agreement is renewable on the same or altered basis, the employee may return to full-time work, or the employee may take full-time retirement. The pension plan changes required IRS review and approval prior to adoption of the partial retirement program.

A participant in the firm's program continues to accrue pension credits. Participation in the program should not have adverse effects on eventual pension benefits from the company's defined benefit plan. For instance, if employees choose to work half-time, they receive pension credits for a half year's employment at their normal full-time pay-rate. If the participants have agreed to demotions in their part-time employment at lower wage rates than their pre-retirement earnings, the pre-retirement earnings form the base from which pension benefits are determined in the final-pay-average formula. Participants are eligible for the same wage increases as full-time workers and promotions may be granted during the contract renewal period.

The program, which was adopted in spring 1980, was specifically designed to give productive employees who do not want to work full-time the opportunity to slow down while receiving pension benefits, allowing the employer to retain valuable skills while offering an opportunity for part-time work to eligible participants.

This body of policies represents an excellent example of an employer's initiative to retain older workers as continuing members of the primary labor force. The program permits the extension of targeted workers' careers by accommodating desires for increased free time without forcing workers into retirement. At the same time, the remunerative package offered to workers offers protection for the worker's standard of living so that an adjustment to part time employment is not matched by an adjustment to reduced income streams.

Phased Retirement and Secondary Production Facilities: Southern Technologies

Southern Technologies is a multinational company specializing in the design and manufacture of electronic components. The firm employs a work force in excess of 10,000.

The company has never experienced difficulty in attracting people to fill its labor needs. Most production jobs are filled by "walk-ins," people who apply for work at the company's employment offices. Engineers are recruited as part of a nationwide program focusing on college graduates, as are other professionals who cannot be drawn from the local labor force.

While most employees are engaged in assembly line work, either putting components together or checking the work of others, all are dependent upon a flow of contracts for continued employment. In periods when the flow of contracts recedes, it is occasionally necessary either to reduce the size of the work force or to transfer workers between production units. Similarly, expansions in demand can call the rapid increases in labor needs and, as a consequence, for capital investment in the creation of work stations at which new employees can do their work. In either case, expansion or contraction, considerable expenses are entailed and employee morale can be adversely affected.

Two distinct mechanisms have been developed to address these inevitable fluctuations in the company's need for labor. The first involves a "back door" phased retirement program, and the second entails a production center called "Over There."

The phased retirement option centers on the switch of older workers from a full-time schedule to part-time work with earnings supplemented through benefits normally associated with retirement.

As a general rule, part-time employment has not played a major role in filling the company's labor needs. A primary impediment to part time work is the high level of investment necessary in the construction of work stations: managers of the firm simply do not feel that the production potential offered by part-time workers justify the expenditures necessary to put them to work. While limited job-sharing has been tried to ameliorate this problem, few of the company's workers follow a part-time schedule. A secondary factor militating against part-time schedules is the firm's practice of labor accounting which focuses on head-counts rather than on full-time equivalent personnel accounting: this practice effectively penalizes managers with part-time labor.

Nonetheless, the firm has encountered a number of situations in which highly valued older workers attracted to retirement were important to various of the company's plans. In an effort to retain these workers' services, the company's personnel office developed a series of personnel and benefit practices which would permit workers to "retire part time" and work part time. Phased retirement in this context is not a personnel offering as much, but instead is best considered a means of "bending the rules" associated with various of the company's personnel and remunerative practices so that these workers' part-time earnings can be supplemented with retirement benefits.

The company's pension plan carries no provision for phased retirement. If a worker is employed in a permanent capacity so that contributions to the pension plan are maintained, no pension benefits can be paid. This is a common provision among pension plans. The company does, however, offer two profit sharing plans which may be disbursed under a variety of circumstances. Included among these are retirement and "financial emergency." If the worker can gain access to part-time work at a necessarily reduced level of earnings, the profit sharing programs' boards of directors have determined that the reduction in earnings represents a financial emergency and qualifies the worker for disbursal of accumulated profit sharing funds. As a result, the worker may enter a form of phased retirement in which reduced earnings are supplemented by a retirement-based income flow in spite of the fact that the pension plan itself carries no such provision.

Few workers have as yet benefited from this practice. Managers familiar with the option believe that limited access to part-time work schedules is a major factor in the program's limited use, but they also believe that selectivity has played a role. Since affected supervisors and managers must approve an individual's access to part time work, it is believed that only the most meritorious workers can access the phased retirement "option." In this sense, the program represents a means of selectively retaining the best older workers past the time at which they would otherwise have retired — a definite advantage for the company.

Southern Technologies' second practice of interest to older workers is "Over There." Over There is a production facility which is located several miles from the main concentration of company facilities. Serving a variety of production functions, Over There employs temporary workers who receive no fringe benefits but who are paid at a rate 10% above equivalent scales for permanent employees. Workers at Over There are free to pursue part-time work schedules and most do.

Over There was originally developed for two reasons. First, it was designed to insulate the firm's primary work force from enforced contractions during slow periods. In addition, workers in the facility could be "pre-screened" and, if appropriate, transferred to the company's permanent labor force.

Over There has surprised its creators with its appeal to older workers. By virtue of its flexibility in scheduling and its total emphasis on monetary remuneration, it has proven very popular among the area's retirees as a place to work. Retirees can, in essence, tailor their schedules around the extent to which they want to work and the social security retirement test to maximize their overall incomes. Moreover, because the pay package is totally monetary, there is no duplication of insurance coverages which would, for many, be duplicative of existing coverages.

An interesting aspect of this appeal to older workers is a high level of participation by Southern Technologies' own retirees. Since workers are temporary and excluded from fringe benefits, retirees may be employed there without violating the restrictions in the company's pension plan described above.

In all, Over There has proven a valuable addition to the company's operation. It has been useful as a protective device in insulating the company's primary work force from economic contractions, and it has proven successful as a production facility. Moreover, it has benefitted the many older workers who have sought and gained employment there.

It is clear that the two employment practices above are directed at quite different groups of workers.

The phased retirement offering is oriented solely to the retention of valued members of the firm's primary work force. The plan permits these workers to remain on the job while enjoying expanded access to the freedom they'd previously identified only with complete retirement. These workers receive the fringe benefits and other privileges associated with permanent employment and are still able to pursue the ends they'd sought through the cessation of work.

Over There, on the other hand, is an explicit attempt at developing a secondary work force. The terms of employment in this facility are more flexible for these workers than for others, though the security of employment is necessarily diminished. In addition, the pay package extended to workers at Over There differs considerably from that offered permanent employees. Again, this practice is consistent with the facility's orientation to a secondary labor force. Together, these factors have contributed to a work place which has proven popular among older would-be workers in general and additionally to a number of the company's retirees.

In summary, it would be inappropriate to suggest that Southern Technologies has developed programs in order to appeal to older workers. Instead, in its phased retirement option and in Over There, the firm has developed programs which serve its own interests and, incidentally, also appeal to a large number of older workers. In each case the interests of the company motivated the programs development and initiation: those older workers who have benefitted have done so because their needs are complementary to those of their employer.

Phased Retirement: Educate Public Schools

One example of the development of an innovative public employer program is the Educate Public School program. This program permits vested employees to retire at age 60 or over while guaranteeing their reemployment in the same job or another job for which they are qualified provided they apply by August of the year in which they are seeking reemployment. Further requirements for eligibility currently include satisfactory medical examination and an above average performance rating. This innovative program, which allows employees to receive their full pension pay-out at the same time they are employed, was the brainchild of the Director of Employment Relations for the district Schools.

In 1978 the Midwest Public Employee Retirement System (MPERS) was altered to eliminate a penalty which reduced pension benefits if a person retired from MPERS but returned to other employment. The intention of the modification was to eliminate the penalty for persons working for other employers, but the change was written so broadly that it actually allowed persons to return to the same job while receiving MPERS benefits. Upon consideration of the new law, the director realized its applicability to the school system and drafted the new policy. On checking with MPERS administrators he found that, while the change was not intended to result in such policies, the school policy was legal under the new law. The policy was adopted by the school board who saw the new policy as costing them nothing while providing a benefit for interested participants.

Unlike other phased retirement programs, the school program was not developed to encourage retirement but instead to keep people working longer and to provide them with more employment options. The changed pension policy is viewed as a benefit to both parties (MPERS and the employee) — providing the employee wishes to have more flexible employment options.

MPERS perceives a possible benefit to the pension system in the following manner. Under MPERS the pension benefit is based on $1\frac{1}{4}\%$ of best salary for each year worked. If a person is age 60 and has worked 20 years, the pension benefit will be 25% of the best salary. If the person worked 10 additional years the pension benefit would be approximately 37.5% of the best salary. Given the high rate of inflation and projected wage increases, the pension beginning 10 years from now is likely to be based on a considerably higher best salary. Thus MPERS, which does not allow accruals after retirement and reemployment, projects that the new program will not be costly to the pension system.

From the employee perspective the new policy may have monetary disincentives if a person is planning on working full-time until retirement, particularly retirement after many additional years of service and assuming wage increases and promotion. But, the system also allows new flexibility. A vested employee wishing to retire at age 60 and return to the same job would begin receiving pension benefits in addition to regular salary. The employee no longer has 4% of their salary deducted from their payroll for pension contributions. In addition, the employee may then choose to switch into part-time work or job-sharing. He or she may also reduce their job responsibilities and salary. The pension benefit would be based on the best salary prior to "retirement" at age 60.

The annuitant is subject to performance evaluations similar to any other employee, but with high performance, is "guaranteed" reemployment until age 70 — the mandatory retirement age. Annuitants who chose permanent part-time employment — including job sharing — are provided with all fringe benefits available to other employees on a prorated basis. These include group health insurance, life insurance, unemployment compensation and disability insurance. Annuitants are not eligible for pension participation. Administrative costs may be slightly higher for the school system for part-time workers but the director states that experience demonstrates that the benefits far outweigh the costs. "Even if the system paid two thirds of the full-time fringe benefits for half-time workers it would still be a bargain." The district's experience with job-sharing has been very favorable — participating teachers have been outstanding performers. The teaming of older and younger teachers — which should increase if more teachers take advantage of the new policy — provides valuable training for the younger team member.

The director firmly believes that the new system provides new beneficial flexibility to older people. He cites as a past example, a high school principal who wanted to slow down as he approached retirement. The principal, at his own request, transferred to the lower positions of junior-high principal and then elementary principal – in essence voluntary job demotions. Unfortunately, while beneficial in providing for the retirement transition, the transfers also adversely affected the employee's eventual retirement benefits. Under the new system, this employee could have "retired" at his highest level and salary and been reemployed in the lower positions. The new options permit considerable latitude for workers to continue in some manner of employment.

Unlike other areas, the school district does not have a teacher surplus. In a few years the director expects there will be a teacher shortage – an event which is already a reality for the industrial arts and math departments due to competition from local aerospace employers. Therefore, the new policy which may encourage teachers to remain in the work force should provide a valuable manpower resource.

Clearly oriented toward maintaining proven workers in the school system's primary labor force, this phased retirement program bears much in common with others discussed earlier and may provide an innovative model for other employers. By allowing individuals to choose the date at which pension benefits begin (after age 60 and 10 years of service in MPERS), combining the benefit with guaranteed reemployment subject to performance evaluations and the option of electing attractive alternative job options, the system may result in individuals choosing to work longer. Because they do not have to retire from their present employer to receive their pension, workers are more likely to continue in employment in a familiar situation. Thus, older productive workers are not forced to seek new employment or subject to the "discouraged worker" syndrome.

The primary disincentive to participation in the program is the inability to continue to receive pension benefit accruals based on increasing salary levels and years of service. But, although they are not eligible for the MPERS retirement system, participants are eligible to contribute to Individual Retirement Accounts (IRA) under current federal law.

The system may also provide a model for policies which encourage continued employment, but do not provide a drain on the social security system. If, the director suggests, the persons who choose to "retire" and elect reemployment do not draw early retirement social security benefits (primarily due to their higher level of earnings and the adverse effects of the SSA retirement test) then their continued SSA contributions would contribute to the financial health of the system. SSA actuarially adjusted delayed retirement credits or delayed retirement bonuses, might further encourage individuals not to apply for social security benefits until they actually retire from their reemployment. At this point it is impossible to predict the behavior of participants, but the policy is an innovative approach to flexible options for older workers.

Phased Retirement: Electro, Inc.

Electro, Inc. is a multinational corporation headquartered in a large, western metropolitan area. Electro, Inc. is a high technology company which serves markets in industry, science, medicine, communications, and defense with a broad range of mechanical components and systems products. The company is in a period of growth: during 1979 500 new jobs were created, and employment at the headquarters site grew by over 10% to a total of approximately 5,500 employees.

In 1976, Electro, Inc. was faced with an acute need for qualified workers. Due to the high cost-of-living in the local metropolitan area, attributable primarily to housing expenses and the expanding labor needs of other employers in the area, the firm confronted — and continues to confront — a tight labor market. Qualified middle-aged or younger workers with families are difficult to attract to the area. Turnover is high as firms with similar labor needs compete for a limited number of workers.

As a response to its personnel needs, Electro, Inc. developed a formalized program of phased retirement designed to retain workers who could retire. Rather than losing retirable workers faced with a choice only between complete retirement or full-time work, the firm sought to retain qualified workers by offering increased work-time flexibility.

The corporate benefits office developed the program as a retirement transition offering. Under the guidelines of this policy — which are considered extremely flexible by management — individuals 60 years of age with 5 years of service can elect to reduce their work week for a 2-year period prior to retirement. Employees voluntarily initiate their participation with a written request at least 3 months prior to their expected entrance into the program. Participants normally retain their prior job classification, but if necessary employees must accept a lower position. Otherwise, the equivalent hourly wage rate continues upon entry into the program.

Employees in the program retain their eligibility for benefit participation on the same basis as regular employees. Where eligible earnings determine the degree of participation, the employee's participation is based on the reduced income level. Since Electro, Inc. has a defined contribution pension plan (offered in conjunction with a profit sharing program) based on earnings, the pension benefits — although reduced along with salary — are not greatly affected.

Conception, review, and adoption of the plan took approximately 1 year. Few, if any, revisions in the originally proposed policy were made in the review processes, and the cost of developing the policy was minimal. Once adopted, the phased retirement program was publicized through the corporate newsletter and magazine, and through managers and supervisors. The firm is currently considering expanding eligibility to age 55 in response to employee's requests.

The program has resulted in the participation of 5 to 10% of eligible employees — mostly skilled workers who otherwise would have retired. Participants appear to like the program and appreciate the opportunity it has given them. Electro, Inc. currently employs approximately 500 workers over age 40, and 75 over 65.

The company has also had a number of retirees return for short-term employment on temporary assignments — usually when the supervisor and the retirees have maintained communication and the opening has been offered and accepted on an informal basis. There is presently no formalized system for cataloging a retiree's skill and willingness to work, although such a program may be introduced in the future.

In general, it seems reasonable to characterize Electro's older worker policies as strongly oriented to the retention of existing workers in the firm's primary labor force. The phased retirement program, a product of considerable planning, arose directly out of labor shortages affecting a pivotal class of positions in the firm. The program itself, while possibly less generous than others described earlier, has nonetheless been successful in luring targeted workers away from retirement and could yet be modified to further improve its appeal.

Annuitant Pools: Western Bankers

Another approach to providing more limited part-time job opportunities for older individuals is the creation of an "annuitant pool" of potential workers by the employer. The establishment of an annuitant pool is an attractive idea which is being implemented by an increasing number of employers across the country. Currently, most existing pools are composed primarily of individuals who occupied positions at the lower rungs of the occupational ladder such as clerical workers. Two descriptions of annuitant pools are presented in the following section.

Western Bankers employs approximately 75,000 workers in 1,100 branches. In Northern California the bank had approximately 4,600 retirees in 1980. In order to take advantage of this potential source of part-time workers the firm introduced a program in 1979 whereby retiring employees were asked if they would consider employment after retirement. Interested individuals complete a card indicating the amount of time they would consider working. The card also lists the employee's job skills, as well as other identifying information. Filed by job skill, the card allows the company to efficiently identify persons capable of filling positions on a part-time basis. Most of the positions are as tellers, clerks and secretaries, but with the exception of managerial positions, virtually all phases of the bank's operations may potentially be filled by the annuitants in the pool. Interestingly, the company maintains this file not only for its own use, but also for those of other client firms who may have a need for such employees.

The annuitant pool is utilized as a labor supply for filling jobs during busy periods, providing vacation relief, and meeting other staff shortages. Retirees returning to or continuing work for the bank under this system are limited to 20 hours per week and are not eligible for fringe benefits other than those accorded to retirees as part of their retirement benefit package. Retirees in the program continue to receive their full retirement benefits. Most retirees contacted do in fact return to fill the positions offered to them. The Southern California Bank affiliate offers a similar program to its retirees.

The annuitant pool established by this employer is an effective personnel tool for use in responding to temporary shortages in a wide range of positions. The workers themselves constitute a trained secondary labor force which is available for efficient application to short-range vacancies, a resource made possible through the protection of pension benefits during times of earnings. That this is a promising approach to solving this problem is evidenced both by the enthusiasm of new retirees in enrolling for the program, by the high rate of acceptances among retirees when temporary positions are offered, and by the firm's continuation and expansion of the program.

The company also offers an employer-provided supplement to Medicare and operates a post-retirement education program through which retirees may receive up to $100 per year for various educational pursuits. The bank has eliminated its mandatory retirement age and pension accruals in the defined benefit plan continue after the normal retirement age of 65. In general, the bank offers benefits which facilitate retirement and promotes part-time, post-retirement work when advantageous to both the employer and the retiree. The annuitant pool offers the bank a potential labor force supply of mature workers with firm specific experience. Utilization of the pool reduces employment service fees as well as training costs, while offering retirees the opportunity to work if they wish to do so.

Annuitant Pools: Insurance Incorporated

Insurance Incorporated is a midwestern company with approximately 8,000 workers in home and field offices. The Company is nationally recognized as a leader in the development of older worker policies. The firm has never had a mandatory retirement policy and approximately 3 to 4% of their workers for the past 25 years have been over 65 years of age. More than 70% of the over 65 workers have been with the company 10 years or more. Most retire voluntarily between ages 66 and 70. In the past 5 years more than 70% of those employees reaching age 65 chose to stay on the job. The company sets performance standards for each job and these standards are the criteria for employment. Age is not a factor. Productive retirees have an option to return to work. Retirees and older current employees receive an in-house newsletter monthly and a local area "Seniors" newsletter.

Retirees are invited to regular functions and have access to employee services. Under the "Rule of 75" — if the age of retirement plus length of service equals 75 or more — retirees are eligible for continued employer provided group insurance coverage with a nominal charge for dependents which includes up to 80% of dental benefits. The firm provides a defined benefit pension plan which allows employees beyond a certain salary level to contribute 4 to 10% of their salary. A supplemental plan based on years of service is also available.

Insurance Incorporated established a temporary workers pool in 1979 to provide temporary full or part-time work assignments to retirees. According to one officer, the pool concept developed as an offshoot of a survey of retirees initiated to provide information prior to the establishment of a preretirement program. The survey disclosed that many retirees missed working. An older woman employee who had just retired at age 75 was in charge of the survey and initiated the idea of the annuitant pool. Once adopted, the participants in the pool became their own best advertisement. Shortly after this adoption, the coordinator received a call at 8 a.m. requesting pool participants to begin a task at 9 a.m. which was expected to take at least two days to complete. The coordinator quickly had 9 people on the job and they completed the task in one to two hours. Reports of this experience quickly circulated throughout the firm and were an important advertisement for the annuitant pool.

Both the company and its retirees benefit from the program. According to one source, the firm is able to obtain highly skilled workers without paying expensive employment agency fees. During the first year of the program, the firm estimated a savings of over $8,000 by using the services of their retirees. Since retirees are already familiar with the company, they need virtually no time-consuming orientation. Most managers prefer pool workers over outside workers because of the retirees' familiarity with the firm, their competency and their enthusiasm.

Each employee is invited to participate in the program as they prepare for retirement. Some employees are not interested at the time but call back later to enroll. Any employee who leaves in good standing is eligible for the pool in the future, and most of the retirees express interest in participating. Each participant is asked to complete a jobs skills form which indicates the days and hours during which he or she will be available to work. On receipt of a manager's request for help, the skills inventory file is reviewed and the appropriate retirees are contacted. The retirees may turn down assignments which are inconvenient. Currently a core group of approximately 25 employees have been utilized frequently. The retirees report benefits in terms of the opportunity to earn extra money and through the feeling of usefulness gained through working.

Retirees are paid weekly by special check. Deductions are not made for federal tax, but state and social security deductions are made. All retirees in the pool recently received a substantial salary increase. Personnel monitors the annuitants' earnings and notifies them when they are nearing the threshold level established by the social security retirement test. They have found, however, that most workers closely monitor their earnings themselves.

Currently most active retirees in the pool are clerical workers, though utilization of workers with higher skill levels has occurred. Broadening the skills utilized through the pool will likely occur as the program becomes firmly established.

Insurance Incorporated's annuitant pool represents perhaps the most polished such offering currently in effect. Not only are terms of employment well suited to potential program participants, but a supportive information function is in place to assist workers in avoiding many of the potential pitfalls of post-retirement work. While it is unusual to find attention of this scale leant to members of a firm's secondary labor force, the potential for expanding the company's existing program suggests its value as a personnel tool.

Annuitant Pools: Midwest Bank

A large bank in the Midwest has organized its own temporary worker pool called the "Ready Work Force." Many of the pool members are senior citizens, including the retirees from the bank. The recruited participants provide the bank with a list of their skills and hours when they wish to work. Most of the workers utilized are clerks, typists, and secretaries although a few professional specialists are included. The participants are paid an hourly wage rate with no benefits. The bank contacts pool members and arranges their temporary placement.

The majority of the "Ready Work Force" are over age 65 and many are over age 70. The bank representative states that the program is successful. It offers the bank a pool of temporary workers – many of whom are familiar with bank operations – without the payment of an employment office fee.

A New Older Workers' Policy: Insure

Insure, a national insurance company employing 2,500 workers over age 55 has recently developed a number of new policies which affect older employees. The company surveyed its older workers in 1980 to determine employees' attitudes concerning work and retirement. The questionnaire included items on planned age of retirement, interest in paid employment following retirement, and preferences for work schedules. The results of the survey, which drew a 79% response, were used to help company policy-makers design effective new personnel and benefit policies.

The survey findings indicated that four out of five of the older employees were interested in paid employment following retirement. The majority desired part-time work for several days a week, and most also preferred to continue working for Insure rather than seeking new employment. The findings also indicated that many older workers had not engaged in pre-retirement planning activities although two-thirds of the respondents were interested in Insure-sponsored pre-retirement programs.

The new policies developed by Insure had several goals: 1) to help older employees and retirees remain in the labor force if they so chose; 2) to help older employees plan for retirement; and 3) to provide community service projects aiding senior citizens.

To retain older workers and provide employment opportunities for retirees, Insure first eliminated their age 70 mandatory retirement age. Next, the company developed a temporary employment program for the firm's retirees. Prior to 1980, retirees could work up to 40 hours a month for the company without losing pension benefits. Under the new policy, employment is computed on an annual basis with retirees able to work up to 960 hours a year, without affecting retirement benefits. Insure's retirees now register with the firm and are called to fill temporary positions for which they are qualified.

Positions range from several days a week to full time and may last for several months. Retirees are paid more than they would receive for similar jobs obtained through employment agencies. The firm uses approximately 60 temporary workers in the home office on an average day.

Insure also identified nearly 300 positions in the home office which could be structured into part-time jobs for retirees. As these positions are vacated, retirees are allowed to move to the jobs on a permanent part-time basis. Many of the positions are suitable for job-sharing by the retirees.

The firm also introduced a training program for typists and secretaries. Workers returning to these positions receive refresher courses and training on the latest office machines.

Finally, Insure developed a voluntary retirement planning workshop for employees 55 years and older. The workshop lasts several hours per week for 8 weeks. Several of the sessions focus on financial topics and include financial planning, savings, and record keeping.

In brief, Insure has developed several different strategies to aid their older workers. To aid the development of their programs, they began with a survey of their older workers' employment preferences. The primary new program provides secondary jobs for retirees. The annuitant pool program is combined with the provision of permanent part-time jobs. The permanent part-time jobs were carefully identified positions within the firm which the program's designers saw as appropriate for part-time work. The two programs provide Insure's retirees with previously unavailable opportunities to maintain their labor force attachments while providing Insure with a pool of skilled, experienced workers. The clerical and secretarial retraining course also helps Insure increase its labor pool for workers in short supply. Overall, the program is a carefully planned attempt to provide retirees with desired options and the firm with experienced employees.

CONTRACT EMPLOYMENT

The employment of older workers as independent contractors appears to offer interesting opportunities to employers in many different industries and employing many different types of workers. Since many older individuals already receive their basic income from public and/or private pension benefits, they may be particularly willing to consider contracts for short-term, part-time work or commission-only opportunities. Such contracts often provide the older individual with an opportunity to continue their participation in the labor force while continuing to enjoy their leisure activities. If employers only request that the individual invest their time in a contract job, and do not require the individual to invest money to buy products, sales kits or other items, the retiree's pursuit of a new career involves only the time he or she invests in it. The following companies have utilized the contract approach in building successful businesses utilizing the older worker.

Protecto, Corporation

Protecto Corporation contracted with 600 new salespersons in 1981 – approximately 135 of them were over age 65. The firm, which sells their products nationwide, has found that older, mature individuals are good sales representatives for its products. The firm has developed the practice of hiring older persons because it is good business. Last year 3 of their top 10 salesmen were over 65. Most of the company's customers, owners of commercial buildings, are themselves older individuals. Mature salespersons appear to have credibility with the customers because of their age and experience.

Protecto recruits its sales personnel through classified advertisements placed in newspapers throughout the country. Due to the firm's favorable experience with older salesmen, they currently advertise for "mature individuals" to sell their products. The contracts with the sales personnel do not specify either a particular sales volume or a definite territory. Depending upon the individual's motivation, he is free to set his own hours and achieve his own goals. The salesperson receives a 25% commission on all sales. Due to its minimal investment in new sales personnel, the firm's management feels it can afford to take risks and give opportunities to individuals who appear to have potential. If the firm had extensive training programs, base salaries and other high initial costs, they would not have been able to take the risks entailed in hiring some of the past sales personnel who have become good producers.

Individual salespersons are eligible for bonus plans and profit-sharing if they achieve a specified sales volume. One of the most effective bonus options for older workers is free to travel to company meetings. Many of the older salesmen have done little or no traveling, and the company sponsored trips motivate them to meet the sales volume required. After they have attended one or two meetings and made friends with other salespersons, peer pressure and the desire to see their friends at the next meeting become important sales incentives. Individuals are also eligible to participate in a profit-sharing retirement plan if they achieve a certain sales volume for 2 consecutive years. Persons over 65 are not eligible for fringe benefits such as group hospital insurance and life insurance.

Many of the older sales personnel are attracted to Protecto by the freedom to set their own hours and their own goals for the job. Most of the company's salesmen work part-time and earn approximately $3,000 to $4,000 a year, but a number of the 65 plus salesmen earn in excess of $40,000 a year in commissions. A 74 year old former pharmacist was recently named "rookie of the year" with total commissions of $45,000. For many of the older salesmen the contract with Protecto provides them with an opportunity to stay active and meet people. Many work only a few hours daily while others work full-time or overtime for sustained periods and then take time off for vacation. A number of the older workers travel throughout several states selling their goods, while others stay near their homes. The flexibility in hours and territory appeals to older individuals who are used to taking responsibility in their jobs.

The receipt of a public or private pension allows many older workers to take the risk involved in accepting a contract with firms such as Protecto. Their primary income source is assured and if the contract sales position does not work out, only their time is lost. Younger workers may find it harder to work on a "commission only" contract due to pressing financial needs. Protecto offers older workers an opportunity to remain in the labor force and establish their own work schedules. Many older individuals have taken advantage of the opportunity and the arrangement has worked out well for the company and the older individuals.

Second Careers: Technology Services

Technology Services is the world's largest technical service organization supplying quality control or quality assurance services. It provides a profit-making model which might be duplicated in other fields. The firm, headquartered in the Los Angeles area, supplies companies such as Ford, Bendix, Amtrak, and others with quality engineers and technical specialists on a full or part-time basis. The business's work force, whose average age is 57 plus is comprised almost entirely of retired persons. The company has approximately 3,500 retirees located throughout the country on their registry and at any time about 300 of them are working.

The company has varied approaches to potential customer firms including direct mail programs, phone, trade shows and newsletters. The central offices work out the major contract with the customer and then contacts a qualified retiree on their roster who lives in the geographical area of the job. The geographical distribution of the retirees greatly reduces travel and living costs which the client company would normally pay their own personnel. Many of the jobs involve developing or advising on the quality control systems of the customer firm's suppliers. The customer uses the services to obtain trained, experienced consultants providing immediate expert help.

The jobs available to different retirees on the roster depend upon their experience as well as the demand in their geographic area. The jobs vary in length from 4 hour jobs to full-time for a year; 90% of them are part-time.

The older employees working through the company are offered a contract to perform a specific job — essentially the firm arranges and schedules jobs which are subcontracted to the retirees. The firm outlines the job, what it is, how much time it will take and the pay. Retirees may refuse jobs and still be offered future contracts. All financial details are handled by the individual. This arrangement allows the retirees flexibility in financial allocations and tax matters. The retirees generally do not receive their pre-retirement level of compensation or responsibility. The retirees utilized generally have an average of 25 years of professional experience, do not require training, and take telephone job instructions.

This company's use of older workers as members of its primary labor force differs from most other company's programs in that workers are addressed as new hires rather than as potential retirees to be retained. In this sense, the company shares with others a motivation to capitalize on the experience of older employees. By concentrating on the attraction of retirees who would be new to the firm, however, this company avoids potential problems associated with simultaneous pension benefits and contributions and with other hazards associated with the rehiring of retirees. Differentiating this program from many others which use older employees as components of the primary labor force is the finite duration of most workers' employment.

Training and Contract Employment: Soft, Inc.

A different approach to utilizing the productive capabilities of older individuals is being pursued by a large northeastern software development firm. Soft Inc. located a computer programming training center in a Florida community with a large retired population. The firm was overwhelmed with applications from older individuals for a limited number of training positions. Those accepted receive a 3 month training course and then work as part-time, independent contractors preparing computer programs for the firm. Management is very impressed by the results of the program — they can tap a growing population of capable workers who appear to be less mobile and more stable than younger workers and who are motivated employees.

The firm plans to expand the program locating additional training centers near retirement communities around the country. Other firms which have similar activities which could be decentralized and located near large concentrations of retired persons may also find advantages in tapping an underutilized sector of the labor force to their mutual advantage.

RETRAINING: HIGH-TEC ENGINEERS

The HIGH-TEC Engineers (H.E.) newly developed training program provides an example of one employer's innovative program for older engineers. Located in the rural northeast, the H.E. Department employs approximately 300 professional engineers in jobs which require almost continuous training due to changing technologies. During the late 70s recruiting engineers for employment became increasingly difficult for the company. At the same time the technology utilized within the Department was undergoing almost constant change. On carefully examining labor supply options, the Department managers decided to invest additional funds in retraining their current older engineers whose skills were becoming technologically obsolete. A cost study demonstrated a 3 to 1 cost/benefit ratio for the department through retraining rather than replacement through new hires. The director states that management also based their retraining decision on its moral responsibilities to offer existing employees the opportunity to upgrade their skill.

High Tec's decision to retrain current employees was based on the belief that, "If we had time to hire new people and familiarize them with our way of doing business, we also had time to retrain people who had contributed to the Department's past success and who were of proven capability and already versed in Department procedures."

In 1977 the company developed three concentrated retraining programs for engineers. Managers were asked to select participants from their departments who were identified as needing skills upgrading and who they perceived as having a chance of getting through and completing the program successfully. Engineers who had kept up to date on their own, including those who had taken advantage of the available H.E. training courses offered outside working hours (typically 5 to 7 p.m.) or the available tuition reimbursements for attending local university classes did not need and therefore were not selected for the new program.

Two of the courses condensed in-plant training sequences which would have taken a year to a year and a half into 10 week half-time and 12 week half-time courses respectively. The employee returned to his or her regular job during the other half day. The third course in Custom Chip Design reduced the time to train from a one year apprenticeship to 6 weeks full-time intensive training followed by 6 months of on-the-job training. By 1980, 40 engineers had participated in the program. Employees received their regular salaries while attending the retraining program.

According to managers the program has been successful in meeting its goal of bringing employees' skills up to current business standards. Initially the selected participants were apprehensive about the program and the reasons for their selection. Once the course was underway, participants were impressed with the opportunity to upgrade their skills and avoid career stagnation. After the initial period, the employees were quite positive about the program. The average age of the participants was 45/46 years and included engineers in their 50s. The courses combined lectures with on-the-job experiences. To complete the course successfully the participants had to design a circuit based on new technology. Only 1 out of the 40 failed to complete this task. He has continued in his old job on programs utilizing older technologies. The successful trainees who completed the courses have been shifted and promoted into new technologies' positions. Although the program initially was developed to teach a specific new technology, the courses now include all new technologies, including microprocessing and integrated circuitry.

The Department's cost analysis shows that the cost of laying off 20 engineers and replacing them with new hires (including idle time and transfer expenses) would have totaled approximately $200,000. The cost of retraining twenty current employees (including unapplied salaries, instructor fees and course development) was approximately $76,000. Thus, the cost of retraining was approximately one-third of the cost of hiring new personnel.

In addition to the dollar cost surveys, the Department was able to provide competent, experienced employees who had contributed to the company in the past with the skills they needed to be productive in the coming decade. The policy provided a positive work climate which instilled renewed confidence in present personnel, and yet ensured H.E.'s capability to meet its business needs.

HIGH-TEC's retraining program presents an unusual approach to retaining older workers in the primary labor force, but one which is consistent in theme with other types of programs. As with a number of other companies' programs, this one recognizes both the value of older workers currently with the firm and the costs associated with their replacement. The product of a highly rationalized planning process, this offering has proven valuable both to the employer and to workers who would otherwise have been lost.

Employment and Remuneration: Investment Associates

Investment Associates is a brokerage firm with home offices in a large western city. Founded in the late 1940s, it employs approximately 300 workers, all of whom occupy white-collar positions. The home office of the firm employs approximately one-half of all employees, while 22 branch offices throughout the far west employ the remainder of the firm's workers.

Of the company's 300 workers, 32 are age 65 or older. In spite of the fact that 11% of the work force exceed the age of eligibility for full social security benefits, only 2 workers had retired between 1978 and 1980, and one of these later returned to the job. The reasons for this high retention of older workers appear to reflect the nature of the firm's labor market, its benefit package, the lack of a mandatory retirement age policy, and the willingness of the firm and its workers to re-negotiate job responsibilities.

The firm offers a range of programatic options which serve the interests of, but are not specifically intended for, older workers. These may be generally treated in terms of remuneration-related offerings involving fringe benefits and employment-related policies defining the parameters within which employees conduct their work.

Insurance and related programs generally available to older workers are varied and predominantly employee funded. Included among these are group coverage for health, life, accident, and long-term disability. Health insurance is provided by the employer for the worker, with the worker paying for dependent coverage. While health insurance is provided for all workers, life and disability coverages are voluntary and entail employee-borne costs. Life insurance coverage is available in amounts based on the employee's salary; the company provides a small amount of coverage without charge, with the employee paying for the remainder through payroll deductions based primarily on age. As with health coverage, life insurance is available to all employees. Accident insurance is available to employees up to the age of 69, and is financed through employee contributions.

Pension coverage is provided through two plans, one of which is oriented to sales (commissioned) personnel, while the second is available to salaried workers. The pension plan for commissioned personnel constitutes a savings-match program whereby an employee may save up to 3.5% of income and realize an equivalent contribution from the employer; while the employee's savings may exceed this level (up to a total of 13.5% of income), the company will not match contributions in excess of 3.5% of employee income. All commissioned employees are covered by this program regardless of age.

The second plan, offered to salaried employees, is a profit-sharing program with annual disbursements based upon company profitability and the employee's salary. Under both plans, employees may borrow up to one-half of their vested balances prior to the age of 65, but full withdrawal may not be accomplished until 65, regardless of the worker's work/retirement status. Those who remain working past the age of 65 continue to participate in their respective pension programs.

The firm offers an unusually large number of employment policies which are widely identified as supportive of older workers, though the practices were not developed solely, or even primarily, for the benefit of this group. Rather, these policies were developed in response to the unique characteristics and demands of the investment industry. This having been noted, it must be added that a large proportion of the firm's older workers have maintained their employment after 65 under altered working conditions offered through these innovative employment policies. Included among these are the absence of a mandatory retirement policy, flexitime, part-time, and increased vacation-sabbatical leaves.

Perhaps most important for older workers is the fact that the firm maintains no mandatory retirement age provision. This is a reasoned policy based on the high premiums associated with experience in this industry. Experience in this context is often strongly associated with sales performance through the accumulation of a clientele and understanding of the market by account executives, and with effectiveness in dealing with the supportive, clerical functions which tend to be unique to this industry. Both characteristics mean extended periods of introduction and training for new hires, and both tend to place a premium on experienced personnel.

The firm offers flexitime schedules, but largely in response to the necessity to monitor and participate in the actions of the New York Stock Exchange; which operates on Eastern Standard Time. In general, flexitime was not developed by this firm as a device to accommodate greater personal flexibility in the daily schedules of individual workers, although this is a side benefit of the policy.

The company additionally offers part-time options to workers when the nature of the position permits. While only 4 of the firm's 32 workers age 65 or older maintain part-time positions, there is no question but that the availability of reduced work schedules is important to them.

The contributions of these policies notwithstanding, two other company policies appear to be of greater importance to the retention of older workers. The first and probably the most important appears to be the policy of distributing accrued profit sharing funds to employees at age 65 regardless of their work/retirement status. Disbursement under both programs is through lump sum payments, so that employees retain flexibility in their determination of how the funds are to be used. Salaried and commissioned employment are not affected by the disbursal of these funds, so that older workers may well derive simultaneous income from pension and from salary or commissions. The ability to derive income from both sources is undoubtedly a factor in the high rate with which workers remain on the job in this firm. While the retirement test as applied under Social Security is acknowledged to be an influence in the decisions of certain employees opting for part-time work, the firm employs a number of individuals over the age of 72 (including their most successful account executive) who draw income from Social Security as well as from their pensions and employment.

Also of importance to the retention of older workers is a readiness on the part of the firm to renegotiate the worker's job responsibilities, and a readiness on the part of at least some workers to take reductions in position. Of the two older workers interviewed during the case study, both had negotiated reduced positions with the company so as to match job responsibilities with their own desires to reduce their work committment. In one case, the reduction in responsibility was brought about by a shift to part-time work, in turn necessitating a shift from a position calling for a full-time occupant. In the second case, this shift involved a lessened involvement in sales activity as an account executive through the partial assumption of activities supportive of another account executive's work. In both cases and in others the alterations in job responsibilities were initiated by the employees, and were negotiated to the mutual satisfaction of worker and firm.

In general, two forces outside the firm contribute to the conditions represented in this case.

1. The firm operates in an industry where experience is an invaluable asset in an employee. Older workers, by virtue of their longevity with the firm, provide the employer a trained labor force.
2. Training costs are high in this industry and workers with requisite skills are simply not available in sufficient quantity in the local labor markets.

These conditions are important factors in the firm's orientation to its older workers.

In summary, it is appropriate to note three general characteristics of this case.

1. First, the company under study faces a tight employment market for highly trained, specialized workers. Because of the high premium placed on experience in the investment industry, older workers tend to be valued employees, both for their own characteristics and for the expense involved in training their replacements.
2. The above notwithstanding, the innovative programs introduced by the company were not implemented for their influences on older workers, nor were older workers considered in the decision to implement the programs. Rather, they were implemented in order to match the requirements of outside activities critical to the company (the New York Stock Exchange being the most important) and to assist in attracting employees generally in a competitive market.
3. Older workers have taken advantage of these programs and of the lack of mandatory retirement policy by remaining on the job in a variety of capacities, some of which are of lesser stature than those positions occupied in the workers' earlier years. As noted earlier, 32 of 300 are 65 years of age or more. Only one net retirement had been realized in the preceding year.

Additionally, three factors appear to be operative in workers' decisions to remain on the job.

1. Continuation of fringe benefits. By utilizing a high incidence of employee contributions in the funding of insurance coverage, the company can offer alternative group coverages to older workers without realizing major costs of its own.
2. Payment of retirement benefits at 65 regardless of retirement status. Payments are made in a lump sum payout which allows workers flexibility in the utilization of the funds. Salary and employment status are not affected.
3. Flexibility with respect to job responsibility and time involvement. It was clear during the case study that the ability to pursue part-time work and to renegotiate job responsibilities allowed a number of workers to stay on the job, though the clear majority of older employees remain in the same full-time positions they pursued during their younger years.

Overall, it appears that older workers answer a need for this employer which can not be addressed handily through the recruitment of workers from other groups. That employees choose to remain on the job rather than retire would appear to be a determinant of flexibility in job assignment and time, continued access to fringe benefits, payout at 65 of accrued pension contributions, and ability to pursue meaningful and often highly remunerative work regardless of age.

Permanent Part-Time: Midwest Bank

A large bank in the midwest has utilized older workers in one part of their operation to alleviate the longstanding personnel problems of turnover, immaturity, and poor work habits in their work force. The check cashing operation in the bank, which handles thousands of checks, offers employment on an hourly wage and with little opportunity for career advancement. The 24 hour, 7 day a week check cashing operation is essentially a "paper factory" which processes a large number of checks per hour. The work force had been composed primarily of young relatively unskilled workers with high turnover rates, problems of immaturity and poor work habits. Management decided that such an operation which handles large amounts of money might benefit from hiring older mature workers who could provide desirable role models for younger workers and contribute to higher standards.

The bank, working with a senior employment agency, has attempted to integrate the work force in this department with a significant number of older part-time workers. A bank personnel officer contacted the senior employment agency, discussed the need for mature workers, outlined the requirements and remuneration for the jobs and generally familiarized the agency with the check cashing operation. Following an initial period of problems in screening and scheduling, the agency directly undertook the tasks of pre-screening older applicants and booking personnel interviews for older applicants with the bank. Accurate descriptions of the job including its speed oriented production nature, the lack of mobility, physical demands and wage levels ($4.18 to $4.90 per hour in spring 1981), improved the quality of applicants placed on the job. The jobs generally require speed in processing checks and standing for long periods. Fringe benefits include vacation and health care in the form of Medicare Supplement. The part-time hours vary from 20 to 40 hours a week and include a choice of shifts. The older individuals primarily work during the day-time shift. The bank's managers consider the part-time jobs as permanent employment and screen applicants from the position who only wish to work part of the year.

Judging from the initial experience, it appears that the placement of older workers in the check cashing operation will help the bank to reduce the absenteeism and turnover. Recruiting a substantial number of older workers has allowed the bank to diversify its work force, improve the quality of job applicants, and upgrade work habits. Currently, the check cashing operation employs 58 persons placed through the senior employment agency.

In instituting the program, the bank has found that the "older old" often do not have the quickness in processing that the job requires. The bank also did not adjust its training program to accommodate the increased age of the new employees. Some training difficulties have occurred. Initially, a number of the older workers had trouble attaining the production standards required. This problem appeared to decrease with time on the job and might have been alleviated through a modified training program which utilized techniques such as self-paced learning and a reduced emphasis on speed.

The social security "retirement test" may complicate the employment of older workers. The bank's spokesman was aware of the regulations of the social security retirement test but did not believe that the bank should monitor earnings for the older beneficiaries. Nevertheless, the manager views the jobs as permanent and is concerned that older individuals have or will quit when they reach the level of income after which their benefits are reduced. Recently, a number of the older employees attempted to refuse a raise in earnings due to the effect of the retirement test on their earnings. The bank granted the wage increase, but it would appear that a method of accommodating employees wishing to "quit" due to the SSA retirement test needs to be instituted. If employees are reluctant to earn over the retirement test threshold, either their hours may be reduced or they may be granted a leave of absence until the next calendar year. Recognition of the retirement test regulations and the development of alternative scheduling arrangements in employment would allow the bank to retain trained, reliable workers while alleviating the anxieties of older workers reaching the threshold level of the social security retirement test.

The utilization of older workers to stabilize high turnover operations and to provide role models of good workers may be effective in many different businesses. The work forces of other operations which offer little career mobility, moderate hourly wages and few fringe benefits may also suffer from problems due to the low education levels of workers, high turnover, absenteeism and unreliability. A substantial number of mature workers in such operations may alleviate personnel problems.

Employment Service for Older Workers: Operation Able

Operation ABLE in Chicago, Illinois provides a successful model for coordination and placement of older workers at a minimum cost. The program takes advantage of the existing not-for-profit senior service organizations in the metropolitan area while providing both a focus and expertise in employment related issues. Operation ABLE (Ability Based on Long Experience) provides a central job bank, job development activities, technical assistance, and other services for the more than 30 senior employment centers. Its purpose is to link interested employers with senior job applicants in the metro area. It also sponsors numerous public relations activities which focus community, media and employer attention on the needs and abilities of older workers. The successful utilization of the media to focus attention on older workers is one of the primary techniques utilized to generate both job listings by employers and applications from older workers.

The 4 year old program's development and success is ultimately due to the energy, intelligence, drive, and hard work of the program's director, Mrs. Shirley Brussell. A former personnel officer, Mrs. Brussell has skillfully built the program through an understanding and sensitivity to employer needs combined with utilization of both the television and newspaper media. Recognizing that appeals to the public service conscience of employers will provide only a limited number of employment opportunities for older individuals, Mrs. Brussell has wisely emphasized the skills and experience that mature older workers may provide employers. Carefully matching employer job needs with applicants enables Operation ABLE to build a satisfied employer base which results in many repeat employer listings and referrals by word of mouth.

Co-sponsorship with a CBS station of an annual metro area job fair attracts many employers and older individuals as well. The job fair is an example of an "event" created by Operation Able which is well-covered by local television and print media. A number of these "events" generate employer and older individual interest in the program.

Mrs. Brussell's talents include the ability to involve, motivate and coordinate many different individuals and organizations. Her recognition of how to provide suitable or meaningful rewards to different groups result in her ability to involve federal, state and local officials in key roles as well as utilizing the abilities of media personalities to provide publicity for older worker employment projects. The skillful utilization of the talents of many different individuals has contributed to the program's success and should be studied by other programs. Instead of making the employment program of older workers a tedious but useful public service, Mrs. Brussell makes the program interesting.

Essentially, Operation ABLE utilizes contacts with employers, job development activities and media coverage to generate employment listings with the program. It operates a job hotline to link interested employers and potential older workers. The "job bank" is kept by the central Operation ABLE office. The job listings are circulated to the most appropriate not-for-profit senior employment centers in the metropolitan area. One of the primary sorting factors utilized in circulating job listings is the geographical location of the employment opportunity. Since many older individuals, particularly those seeking part-time work and/or relatively low wage positions, are seeking employment within an easy commuting distance from their homes, high priority is given to providing listings at the senior centers nearest the job site. Operation ABLE concentrates on job development and the primary task of the network agencies is to match their applicants with the listings provided by the central office. In the first 9 months of 1980, the ABLE network agencies placed 3,682 older workers in jobs.

One of the primary obstacles to developing an Operation ABLE style network is that the not-for-profit agencies vary in their emphasis and their employment expertise. Many agency personnel may have little knowledge of job development skills, employment interview techniques, and other employment-related subjects. In an attempt to ease the problems related to lack of knowledge on employment issues by network agencies, Operation ABLE has provided technical assistance and training for personnel from the network agencies. In 1980, the program conducted 40 training workshops as well as site visits and consultations. A monthly newsletter, *NETWORKING,* is circulated to participating agencies.

The need for trained personnel and evaluative mechanisms for participating network agencies is an important link in developing a successful program based on this type of model. Untrained personnel in the not-for-profit agencies may jeopardize the success of the program by failing to fill vacancies, failing to screen older applicants for appropriate openings, failing to match applicants with the appropriate job openings, and other shortcomings. The central agency must develop effective training programs and conduct on-going evaluations of the placement rates, durations of placements, and satisfaction of employers with the different network agencies. Employers who list openings and then receive no response or who have inappropriate applicants referred for the job may elect not to list further openings and/or discuss their negative impressions of the program with other employers. Alternately, older workers who contact the central office and are referred to a participating agency which fails to follow-up on their application or in other ways fails to place them appropriately, may drop through the "holes" in the network. An effective Management Information System is important to the success of a decentralized organizational model such as Operation ABLE.

The centralization of the employment functions in the Operation ABLE model allows the program to operate successfully on the efforts of only a handful of employment specialists. Although additional funds for training network agency staff members would enable the program to expand further and develop more jobs and successful placements, the existing program provides an example of a successful model operated with only minimum funding.

In some cases the operation ABLE works directly with employers rather than going through the not-for-profit agencies. If an employer has a particular interest in employing older workers in an ongoing program, Project ABLE may recruit, screen, place and evaluate older workers for the employer. This experience is valuable to the central office personnel in familiarizing them with specific employer needs, the problems of placements and the experience of screening and matching older workers with jobs. The direct placement service is an outcome of active job development activities. The employer may not have originally intended to target older workers as a particular resource group. Following consultations with Project ABLE staff and perhaps experimentation with employing a small group of older workers, employers may identify older workers as a potential employment group which would meet their needs. If appropriate, the central Operation ABLE staff may plan and administer a program to place older workers in the employer's organization.

Summary: Although many older individuals may be interested in finding employment, it is often difficult for them to find suitable jobs. Conversely, the skills and experience of older workers may be valued and desired by employers, but it may be difficult for them to locate appropriate individuals for their positions. Employment services such as Operation ABLE may be needed to match older workers with jobs and to increase demand for older workers through media exposure. The model provided by Operation ABLE may be replicated in other areas. The development of a central employment service utilizing local senior centers provides economic and service advantages which may be of interest to policy-makers attempting to develop placement services for older persons.

CONCLUSION

The examples of innovative programs for older workers described in the preceding section may provide models which can be adapted by many other employers in varied employment settings. Success in retaining, retraining, and attracting "new" older workers frequently depends on designing programs which meet the preferences of older individuals for employment and income. Simply altering one segment of the work experience, such as hours of work, may not result in the development of effective programs. Organizational policies, such as "head count budgeting," may retard the success of programs promoted by upper level management. If lower level managers are penalized through the budget for hiring or retaining part-time workers, they are likely to stick to full-time employees. The consideration of older workers in the full range of human resource planning may effect all human resource activities. It is clear from the available research studies on older workers that a uniform time modification program, for instance, will not affect all older workers equally. Different individuals in different types of jobs may desire modifications based on their positions. Programs which are effective and appealing to managers may not be attractive to blue-collar workers. We cannot be certain that what we know now concerning job preferences, hours, etc. will hold true into the future. Managers will need to periodically assess the preferences of employees and evaluate the extent to which programs are meeting worker's needs. Periodic surveys and other feedback mechanisms will enable human resource managers to adjust their policies to a changing labor force.

Economic and demographic realities are likely to change the plans of both older workers and their employers. Continued inflation, for instance, is likely to force many older workers to choose to remain in employment. Since federal legislation prohibits mandatory retirement prior to age seventy and changes in the social security system are likely to encourage later retirement ages, employers will need to carefully examine their policies to be in the position to accommodate the changing work force. Failure to anticipate and plan for the possibility of an older work force is likely to disrupt the best laid human resource plans. On the other hand, beginning early to consider alternative career plans for employees, retraining obsolescent workers, developing plans for lateral transfers, instituting part-time work or phased retirement programs, and considering job modification programs will enable an employer to build flexibility into the structure of its jobs. Such flexibility will enable an organization to retain the skills of its older workers while providing promotional opportunities for other workers. Effective programs will likely satisfy the preferences of older workers for increased leisure time while providing employment opportunities.

FOOTNOTES

1. William A. Mercer, Incorporated. *Employer Attitudes: Implications of an Aging Work Force.* New York: William Mercer, Inc., 1981.

6
Discussion
and
Policy Implications

INTRODUCTION

Mounting public pension costs, shifting demographic trends leading to changes in the composition of the population, a biomedical revolution contributing to increased life expectancies, inflation and a host of other factors have resulted in a growing interest in the labor force participation rates among older workers and retirement patterns. Projections of the costs of supporting expanding numbers of retirees through the next 50 years have focused attention on employer, organized labor, and government policies which encourage the labor force withdrawal of older workers. Research is also beginning to examine preferences for employment or retirement among older citizens.

Retirement patterns in the past decade have shown a continuation of trends established in prior years. At best, recent data demonstrate that the trend toward early retirement may be slowing down, but as yet no evidence exists to suggest that the trend has leveled off or reversed. Labor force participation rates of persons 65 and over have remained relatively stable for the past several years at approximately 20%. Despite high inflation rates and the ADEA Amendments of 1978, the large majority of older persons are continuing to retire at or before the age of 65.

Raising the mandatory retirement age to 70, in itself, does not appear to have had a significant effect on retirement behavior. Contrary to opinions expressed by many advocates, it does not appear that large numbers of older workers will choose work over retirement if only provided the opportunity today. Rather than being barred from work, most individuals appear to be "opting out" for a variety of reasons related to individual preferences and the effects of complex sets of public and private policies which impose disincentives to continued employment.

Continuation of present retirement trends combined with the almost unpredictable lengthening of the lifespan brought about through medical advances may well present very serious retirement funding problems in the future. The availability of money to support unproductive members of the society is ultimately tied to the state of the national economy. It is reasonable to predict the American economy will not continue to sustain the rapid growth of former years. It is no longer reasonable to expect future growth alone to bear the expected costs of maintaining growing adult dependency ratios.

If current patterns continue — including early retirement, high inflation, and low levels of individual savings in support of retirement — older citizens in the U.S. may face difficult problems in the future. Swollen ranks of retirees demanding a larger slice of a stable or declining pie are likely to meet increasing resistance — especially if many of those retirees voluntarily terminated work prior to declines in their productive abilities. An equally unattractive alternative would have retirees forcibly bearing a steadily deteriorating standard of living. In light of these ramifications of continuing current practices, it would seem appropriate to explore and test other approaches to employment and retirement among older individuals. One such alternative involves the establishment of new institutional frameworks which at a minimum encourage a longer working life for older workers. To do otherwise is to ignore the obvious challenges of the near future. The options now open to government, labor and private employers are very broad — the number of reported workers past 65 is sufficiently small to experiment. There remains time to test hypotheses concerning worker reactions to alternative work options, remunerative packages, and tax policies. Experimentation with these and other policies, however, must be started immediately. To develop, adopt, implement and evaluate policies takes time. The longer government, organized labor, and private employers wait, the more limited will be the choices available.

Major modifications in retirement related policies must, in a number of ways, break with tradition. They must cast aside existing myths relating to older workers themselves and to the potential for older workers to inflict negative impacts on their younger colleagues and on the employers for which they work. Additionally, because organized labor has long argued for earlier and earlier withdrawals from the labor force, moves toward extended worklives must be led by forces which have in the past followed the leads of organized labor. Moreover, since organized labor is not advocating the extension of the worklife or alterations in personnel or remunerative packages which make such an extension more desirable, the proposed modifications will be more difficult to accomplish. Each of these issues merits discussion, for each influences the context within which issues surrounding retirement and the extension of the worklife must be addressed.

Age Discrimination

Many advocates of older workers have freely utilized the term "discrimination" in explaining group differences in income between younger and older workers. While clear examples of discrimination have been enumerated in many such discussions, advocates have sometimes overlooked the effect of human capital differences, geographic and industrial factors, and a host of other influences on group income differentials.

Age is one of many sorting devices used by employers in the past few decades, in part because of the high cost of developing individualized methods. Age is an easy criterion to use. Although performance appraisal systems which rate an individual's ability to perform a job result in more equitable sorting procedures, the high cost of developing effective systems has discouraged their widespread implementation. The use of age-based devices has resulted in the undervaluation of many effective older workers, as well as promoting the effective termination of unproductive older individuals. However, two developments of recent years — growing interest in issues related to older workers and the increasing adoption of innovative employment practices devised to appeal to older workers — suggest that many employers are beginning to discard their former reliance on age-based policies and decisions. Age discrimination legislation and increasing media attention on the effects of demographic shifts in the population have contributed to an increased awareness of age-related issues. The aggressive recruitment of older workers by employers confronting labor shortages suggests that assumed reductions in productivity related to age are not sufficiently large to influence employers confronting staffing problems. In short, employers' "tastes for age discrimination" apparently disappear quickly in the face of labor shortages and declining numbers of younger workers. These trends suggest that age discrimination as a common practice may be reduced considerably in the next decades as the rapid decline in new job entrants affects the economy.

Employers

Employers are a remarkably flexible group. Over the years, those businesses which have lasted have been able to do so only through the continual and occasionally dramatic adoption to change. This flexibility notwithstanding, employers do not operate in a vacuum. National policy relating to a myriad of issues delimits the ranges of options available to business. Just as directly, the raw materials available to business constrain the uses and technologies applied to those resources. In both cases, the issues described in earlier chapters will — must — change the orientation of employers toward the older segments of their labor force.

At issue are a number of very fundamental aspects of personnel policy. With ever-earlier retirement as the norm, a number of important questions have simply not required asking. What working conditions best suit older workers? What pay packages best motivate them? What sort of career track is best for a 58-year old worker who will be with the company for 12 more years? How do all of these issues relate to productivity? These are fundamental questions — ones which have long since been satisfactorily resolved for employees in younger age groups. One of many major challenges facing business in the next two decades is, simply, what to do with these workers about whom so little is known.

Older Workers and Job Availability

Suggestions that the availability of employment for youth, women, and minorities are affected by the retirement behavior of older workers are many and have been made for many years. Whether reflected in the availability of jobs for the jobless or in promotional opportunities for other labor force components, encouraging retirement to "make room" for other workers, has been seen as a viable employment strategy for decades. Based largely on what is sometimes termed the "lump of labor" theory, the rationale underlying these arguments suggests that a fixed and limited number of jobs exist in the economy, and that exits from employment contribute largely to the availability of openings through which entry is possible. There is reason, however, to question this approach. First, economic theory suggests that the relationships between retirement and employment opportunities are not so well defined: in fact, to the extent that continued employment generates additional disposable income, there is reason to suggest that exactly the opposite association prevails. Additionally, there is no clear evidence that individuals in the American labor force perceive older workers as bottlenecks to the employment opportunities available to others. The authors found that vast majorities of employers in a nationwide survey did not perceive any negative impact on other labor force subgroups as a result of the ADEA Amendments. Several studies have concluded that workers themselves do not believe that older workers should retire to "make room for other workers." Other research has generated similar conclusions. Even in clerical jobs where potential competition between members of older and younger age groups is most likely to surface, little pressure is anticipated. For other occupations, the potential adverse effects of delayed retirement on younger age groups is insignificant.

Although there is apparently no immediate effect on other labor force subgroups from the retention of older workers, within the next two decades there is likely to be growing pressure from the middle aged "baby boom" cohort to retire older workers who block avenues of promotion. By 1990, over 50% of the labor force will have moved into the 25 to 44 year age group. Sharp competition will occur for limited numbers of positions at higher organizational levels. Anticipated problems will center around the opportunities for progression, and employers will face pressures to accelerate early retirement by adding further inducements, or to develop programs involving the lateral transfer and demotion of older employees. Employers beginning now to develop alternate career plans for their employees may avoid major problems later.

The Perspective of Organized Labor

During the past 50 years organized labor has been in the forefront of the movement which has altered the work-leisure trade-off of American workers. Organized labor has often served as the conduit to management in expressing employees' preferences on issues such as personnel policies, hours of work, and pension benefits. Collective bargaining has provided the framework through which many new policies have been developed, and benefits gained by unionized employees have become models for other employers' policies.

Paradoxically, in the current debate over policies conducive to the retention of older workers, many labor unions have expressed opposition to the introduction of options which could promote this end. Organized labor does not appear to be sensitive to the desires of many older workers to continue in employment, or to the critical problems which may arise in public and private pension plans as large numbers of workers exit from the labor force at earlier and earlier retirement ages. The answer to problems associated with older workers and retirement as enunciated in this quarter of the economy is apparently to provide higher retirement benefits — hopefully including automatic cost of living increases — for workers retiring at younger and younger ages.

In an ideal society, these solutions might in fact be optimal for many individuals — although others would apparently desire to continue working regardless of retirement income. Unfortunately, unions' solutions are expensive and, particularly automatic cost of living increases, would introduce an unpredictable liability into the private pension systems which may well be impossible to meet later. Aside from the questionable equity of requiring younger workers to finance the leisure years of healthy and productive people who have chosen to withdraw from the labor force, the overall costs of such programs in light of the projected demographic changes would be extremely high in the future.

The lack of union interest and support is likely to slow the adoption of many innovative policies for altering retirement behavior — especially among firms with unionized labor forces. The absence of an organized mechanism for presenting the preferences of workers and for developing programs which would satisfy the needs of potential retirees contributes to the "hit and miss" style with which existing programs have been adopted. Lacking formal lines of communication, employers are often unaware of employee preferences which might influence the development of new policies. Employers also frequently lack information on the progressive policies of other employers which might be adopted by their own companies. Consequently, progressive companies are frequently attempting to develop such policies "in the dark." If organized labor were to rethink this approach to older worker issues, its contributions would provide valuable communication networks and leadership in the development of difficult policy options.

In the absence of major shifts in the policies of organized labor, employers and government must take the lead in reappraising policies affecting retirement and the employment of retirable workers. This reappraisal must focus both on limiting the constraints facing the workers themselves, and on the constraints which limit the degree to which public and private policymakers may redefine the terms of employment.

The concluding pages of the chapter discuss modifications in existing policies which might be adopted by public and private employers as well as by federal policymakers.

POLICY RECOMMENDATIONS

Policymakers in both the public and private sectors can do much to shift the burden of incentives and disincentives surrounding the retirement decision. Employers in both the private and the public sectors face two fundamental alternatives.

1. They can continue present early retirement incentives which encourage still capable workers to leave the labor force — the "do nothing" approach;
2. They can remove present disincentives to work from public and private pension systems while experimenting with work options and remuneration plans which encourage continued labor force participation — e.g. eliminate work disincentives while allowing or encouraging individuals to make their own decisions concerning employment.

In addition, federal policymakers have a third alternative which would influence the success of employer policies in retaining older workers.

3. Raising the age of early and normal retirement under the social security system while providing incentives within the system for older individuals to continue in employment.

The first option, continuation of present policies, is certainly the easiest and, in the short run, the option which would generate the least controversy. In the longer run, however, neither firms nor the nation will benefit from this course of action.

The second and third options facilitate the lengthening of worklives — indeed, the third option effectively mandates it. The two are not mutually exclusive and, very possibly, should be implemented concurrently.

Raising the Age of Social Security Eligibility

Raising the age of early and normal retirement — the ages at which social security benefits are available at full and reduced levels — is supportable on a number of grounds. From a purely financial perspective, the entry of increasing numbers of individuals into retirement and their longer life-span within retirement will continue to add considerably to the cost of providing old age and survivors' benefits. While the financial health of the social security system is determined by the state of the economy as well as the relationship between retirees and active labor force participants, the growing beneficiary-to-worker ratio will produce a requirement for taxes around the year 2000 which will be untenable under current financing mechanisms. While alternative financing schemes could be employed to shift the burden of this need for revenue among various elements of the labor force, the liability itself will remain intact unless the number of retirees can be reduced. Moreover, the relative protection accorded social security revenues from other competing uses under its current independent financing mechanisms could very possibly be lost in a shift to alternative financing schemes. The gradual extension of ages of eligibility for social security benefits would — by reducing the number of years most individuals collect benefits and lengthening the time during which revenues are collected — both reduce the programs liabilities and expand its revenues.

Moreover, improvements in morality rates in recent decades have extended the life expectancy of U.S. citizens. According to current mortality tables, 3 years can be added to the worklife of 65 year old Americans without reducing the average period of retirement below that which existed at the time the social security program was introduced. In short, extending the worklife need not rob citizens of full and rich periods of retirement.

Finally, if ceilings in the ability to derive revenue are acknowledged and if the ranks of retirees swell as has been predicted, only the reduction of benefits will permit the continuation of present retirement patterns. This is not an attractive alternative. The creation of a large elderly population living in poverty should not be an objective of present policies of the nation or of its employers.

If the ages of eligibility for social security benefits are to be changed action must be taken soon. The social security programs constitute a social contract. Despite confidence shaken by reports of potential bankruptcy and despite initial problems in administration of the SSI program, the performance and predictability of the Social Security Administration and its programs have earned the high esteem of the American public. The continuation of this esteem in the future is predicated upon its continued predictability. Potential major modifications in the system must be communicated long before they are implemented. The ages of eligibility for social security benefits should be raised around the turn of the century through legislation adopted in the near future. Parallel programs should be strengthened to assure that those who must withdraw from the labor force early for reasons of health will not be adversely affected by this change in policy.

The need to act quickly in the implementation of this policy cannot be overstated. The long transition period necessary to allow individuals to center retirement plans around new retirement ages is essential to the viability of the modifications. Recent administration proposals to decrease social security benefits received after early retirement illustrate the political impracticality of attempting to change benefits within short time frames. People approaching retirement age or who have already retired will strongly resist changes which affect their retirement income. Such proposals introduce unnecessary anxieties among older individuals and result in a hostile atmosphere in which any proposed changes are likely to be resisted. A carefully conceived program involving only long-term changes is more likely to be acceptable.

The long transition period constitutes a blessing. It permits the initiation, testing, and final implementation of policies and programs which may complement and reduce the need for shifts in social security eligibility criteria. These shifts in policy, associated both with the public and private sectors, correspond to the second alternative identified above — the removal of disincentives to continued work for older individuals. Policy recommendations supportive of this end are presented in the following pages.

Altering the Balance of Incentives and Disincentives to Work and Retirement

Chapters 3 and 4 of this book discuss in detail the incentive structure surrounding employment among older workers. The policy recommendations which follow are distilled from these discussions.

- *Public policymakers should alter or eliminate the social security retirement test.* The retirement test is a clear disincentive to employment among pensionable workers. If the elimination of the retirement test is not feasible at this time, a demonstration project evaluating the impact of the elimination of the retirement test should be funded. A demonstration project, if carefully designed and evaluated, would provide a realistic assessment of the impact of elimination of the retirement test. Existing studies are subject to severe limitations imposed by data problems and narrow assumptions.

- *Public and private policymakers should promote the extension of actuarial pension adjustments to workers continuing in employment past the normal retirement age.* Adjustments of lesser scale force additional costs of employment on older workers and promote retirement. Moreover, the provision of actuarial adjustments to benefits available and funded at the normal retirement age does not impose significant costs on employers over liabilities incurred if retirement occurred at the normal retirement age.

- *Public and private policymakers should promote the universal extension of pension accruals reflecting service and earnings increases generated after the normal retirement age.* Already widely adopted in the private sector, these provisions would remove present disincentives to work among older workers.
- *Public officials should alter the rates employed in the Early Retirement and the Delayed Retirement Adjustments in the social security system.* Early retirement adjustments approaching actuarial levels combined with present delayed retirement adjustments at one-third of the actuarial rate constitute both an incentive to early withdrawal from the labor force and a disincentive to delayed retirement. At a minimum, the social security system should provide actuarial adjustments for persons working past age 65, though this point becomes moot if the retirement test is dropped.
- *Public and private policymakers should promote the establishment of remunerative mechanisms which allow workers to "retire" gradually.* Programs which allow workers to simultaneously reduce the number of hours worked while drawing pro-rated pension benefits are currently experimental. The extension of this type of opportunity may promote the lengthening of the worklife of older individuals.
- *Public and private policymakers should develop programs which allow workers to enjoy tax advantages in the deferral of earnings for eventual retirement.* Expansion of IRA and Keough limitations and the generation of similar mechanisms for individuals with pension coverage will promote savings for retirement and reduce reliance on public and private pension systems. Such programs would also allow older workers to derive greater satisfaction from remunerative packages.
- *Public and private policymakers should promote the development of more flexible remunerative benefit packages which allow workers to select fringe benefits most important to their needs.* Complete flexibility in benefit selection has proven unpopular in the private sector due to high costs. Limited flexibility, in conjunction with a core of universal benefits, would allow workers to enhance the perceived value of benefits at limited additional cost to employers. Such changes may require amendments to the ADEA Amendments of 1978.

- *Public and private policymakers should simplify the complex system of laws and policies which affect the labor force participation and withdrawal of older individuals.* Employers are swamped with legally derived and enforced parameters. The complexities of existing legislation force undue costs on many employers – particularily small employers without formal personnel systems. Expansive bodies of policy, both public and private, demand simplification and meaningful dissemination to individuals.

- *Public and private policymakers should encourage and provide greater flexibility in the hours of work.* Particular emphasis should be placed on the development of permanent part-time jobs in all occupations, at all levels of the career ladder, and in all industries. Flexible work arrangements should be carefully structured in a manner which will not reduce the eventual retirement benefits of participating workers.

- *Public and private policymakers should develop and implement non-age related training and promotional opportunity policies.* Contrary to mythology, research demonstrates that older workers do not lack the ability to learn new skills or to undertake new jobs. Training programs for older workers should be designed to meet the learning needs of this population, incorporating such techniques as self-paced learning.

- *Public and private policymakers should develop and implement effective employment transition programs for older workers.* Such programs should provide job counseling, placement services, training for second careers, job development and job transition support for older persons. Many older workers and retirees require assistance in obtaining new full or part-time jobs. Presently, most public manpower programs do not adequately serve or understand the specific job-related needs and abilities of older workers. Successful programs should be examined, and specific information on those programs should be widely disseminated to serve as models for other programs.

- *Public and private policymakers should carefully examine existing and developing progressive policies and programs which encourage the continued employment of older workers. Information on successful programs should be widely disseminated.*

Such information should include, if possible, the costs and benefits of the program, the older worker and employer perspective on the program, methods through which the program may be adapted to fit other employer's needs, the success of the program in altering retirement behavior, and other factors.

- *Public organizations should develop and disseminate labor market information by age classes within different occupations and industries.* Such information should be made available in a labor-market specific basis.

- *Public and private employers should project future labor supply needs against projections of labor force supply.* The projection of future human resource needs in combination with projections of potential labor force supply may alert employers to potential problems. Given sufficient time, program and policy alterations could reduce future labor force bottlenecks.

- *Public and private organizations should sponsor research on older worker and retirement issues which have been highlighted in previous chapters.* The development of effective programs which result in older workers continuing in employment must be based on useful information concerning the desires of older persons. Research on such issues as fringe benefit preferences, the effectiveness of delayed retirement bonuses and other issues is necessary if new programs and policies are to be successful.

CONCLUSION

It is the authors' opinion that the 1980s will initiate a period in which the implementation and adoption of new personnel and remuneration policies will occur through a more deliberate, planned process. The initiation of new policies is likely to occur on a more rational, systematic basis as demographic changes begin to enter the time horizons of employer planning periods and as the media provides more information on the impact of demographic shifts in the work force as well as information on innovative employers' policies. Additional experience will reveal which policies are appropriate in which operational contexts, as well as information about the preferences of workers. In the final analysis individual firms will — and must — determine the feasibility of profitably implementing necessary strategies in the vast range of industrial settings which comprise the national economy.

Yet private firms cannot undertake this task alone. Government is a powerful force in restraining the options available to employers and in shaping the incentives surrounding the options of workers. It is essential that government neutralize or reverse the incentives which now drive workers into retirement. It is also essential that government join with business in the exploration of policy alternatives consistent with the public interest, with the individual rights of workers, and with the continued economic viability of employers.

As suggested earlier, the ages of eligibility for social security benefits should be delayed and private and public efforts to make continued employment attractive to older persons should be expanded. The two strategies complement one another well. First, the Social Security Administration's financing is presently precarious and projected future trends suggest that the problems are just beginning. Second, the economy will need the skills of productive older workers. While the national labor market will not feel the full force of the demographic shifts cited in Chapter 2 until late in the century, increasing numbers of firms and industries are experiencing labor shortages due to current retirement patterns. Many of these firms are attempting to develop programs which retain the skills of older workers. Older workers, for their part, have indicated an interest in retaining a place in the labor force if the conditions of employment can be changed. In short, there is every reason to suspect that the recommendations cited in the preceding discussion can meet with success now.

There is much we do not know about retirement. Thoughtful analysis and discussion aside, we simply do not have much experience in the successful modification of employment practices to appeal to older workers. Neither have we generated sufficient information on alternatives to the prevailing practices. Yet, the widespread adoption of policies capable of meeting future needs may still be undertaken on a small scale and in experimental contexts. Sufficient time remains to learn the game before the stakes are raised.

Bibliography

Allen, Robert E. and Douglas K. Hawes. "Attitudes Toward Work, Leisure, and the Four Day Workweek," *Human Resources Management,* Spring 1979.

American Council of Life Insurance. *Pension Facts 1978–1979,* American Council of Life Insurance, 1979.

Anderson, Joseph M. *Modeling Analysis for Retirement Income Policy,* Washington: Employee Benefits Research Institute, 1980.

Anschell, Susie. *Potential for Semi-Retirement in Public Agencies: A Survey of Active and Retired Staff,* final report, Seattle, Washington, Institue of Governmental Research, University of Washington, March 1980.

Balch, B. W. "The Four-Day Week and the Older Worker," *Personal Journal,* December 1974.

Barfield, Richard and James Morgan. *Early Retirement: the Decision and the Experience,* Ann Arbor: University of Michigan, 1969.

Belbin, R. M. *Training Methods for Older Workers,* Paris: Organization for Economic Cooperation and Development, 1965, cited in Irvin Sobel, *Employment: Background and Issues,* Washington D.C.: 1971 White House Conference on Aging, March 1971.

Best, Fred. "Recycling People: Work-Sharing Through Flexible Life Scheduling," *The Futurist,* February 1979.

_____. "The Future of Retirement and Lifetime Distribution of Work," *Aging and Work,* Summer 1979.

_____. and Barry Stern. "Education, Work, and Leisure: Must They Come in That Order?" *Monthly Labor Review,* July 1977.

Bloom, Gordon F. and Herbert R. Northrup. *Economics of Labor Relations,* Fifth Edition, Homewood, Illinois: Richard D. Irwin, Inc., 1965.

Boskin, Michael J. "The Long-Run Social Security Financing Problem and Retirement Behavior," testimony presented to Subcommittee on Oversight, Committee on Ways and Means, U.S. House of Representatives, September 10, 1980.

Burkhauser, Richard. Written testimony to the Subcommittee on Oversight of the Committee on Ways and Means, U.S. House of Representatives, Hearings on Work, Retirement and Social Security, September 10, 1980.

Byrne, James J. "Occupational Mobility of Workers," *Monthly Labor Review,* February 1975.

Calvasina, Eugene J. and Randy W. Boxx. "Efficiency of Workers on the Four-Day Workweek," *Academy of Management Journal,* September 1975.

Cantrell, Stephen R. and Robert L. Clark. "Retirement Policy and Promotional Prospects," unpublished paper, North Carolina State University, Raleigh, N.C., undated.

Chapman, J. Brad and Robert Otterman. "Employee Preferences for Various Compensation and Fringe Benefit Options," in William F. Glueck (ed.), *Personnel: A Book of Readings,* Dallas: Business Publications, Inc., 1979.

Chinoy, Ely. *Automobile Workers and the American Dream,* New York: Random House, 1955.

Clark, Robert. *Adjusting Hours to Increase Jobs,* Special Report #15, A Special Report of the National Commission for Manpower Policy, September 1977.

_____. "Early Retirement Incentives and Government Policies," Testimony Prepared for the Subcommittee on Oversight, Committee on Ways and Means, U.S. House of Representatives, September 10, 1980.

Cohen, Allan R. and Herman Gadon. *Alternative Work Schedules: Integrating Individual and Organizational Needs,* Massachusetts: Addison-Wesley Publishing Co., 1978.

Colvin, Walter. *Alternative Work Schedules Survey – Manhattan Central Business District.* Prepared by the Port Authority of New York and New Jersey Planning and Development Department, September 1980.

Congressional Research Service. "Background Material on Work, Retirement, and Social Security," Washington D.C.: U.S. Government Printing Office, 1980.

Cooper, Forrest, Jr. "Acquiring Technical Competence: New Hires or Retraining Present Personnel," New York: General Electric Company, 1980.

Copperman, Lois A. "Alternative Work Policies in Private Firms," *The Personnel Administrator,* October 1979.

_____. "The Labor Market and Older Workers: the Changing Employer Perspective," paper prepared for the Gerontological Society, San Diego, California, November 1980.

_____ and Fred D. Keast. "In the Wake of ADEA," final report for the President's Commission on Pension Policy, Portland, Oregon: Institute on Aging, Portland State University, February 1980.

_____, Fred D. Keast, and Douglas G. Montgomery. "Older Workers and Part-Time Options," *Personnel Administrator,* October 1981.

Copperman, Lois F. and Anna M. Rappaport. "Pension and Welfare Benefits for Older Workers: the Preliminary Impact of the ADEA Amendments," in *Aging and Work,* Spring 1980.

Cramer, James C. "Fertility and Female Employment: Problems of Causal Direction," *American Sociological Review,* April 1980.

Daatland, Svein Olav. "Flexible Retirement in Industrial Companies," *Aging and Work,* Summer 1980.

Dalton, G. W. and P. H. Thompson. "Accelerating Adolescence of Older Engineers," *Harvard Business Review,* 1971.

Derthick, Martha. *Policymaking for Social Security,* Washington, D.C.: The Brookings Institution, 1979.

Deutermann, William V. and Scott Campbell Brown. "Voluntary Part-Time Workers: A Growing Part of the Labor Force," *Monthly Labor Review,* June 1978.

Drucker, Peter F. "Old Consumers vs. Young Producers," *Wall Street Journal,* December 18, 1979.

_____. *Managing in Turbulent Times,* New York: Harper and Row, 1980.

Dunlop, John T. "The Limits of Legal Compulsion," *Labor Law Journal,* February 1976.

Employee Benefits Research Institute. *Retirement Income Policy: Considerations for Effective Decision Making,* an EBRI Issue Report, Washington D.C.: Employee Benefit Research Institute, 1980.

Elbing, Alvar O., Herman Gadon, and John R. M. Gordon. "Flexible Working Hours: It's About Time," *Harvard Business Review,* January-February 1974.

Fleisher, Dorothy and Barbara Hade Kaplan, "Characteristics of Older Workers: Implications for Restructuring Work," in Pauline K. Ragan (ed.), *Work and Retirement: Policy Issues,* Los Angeles: University of Southern California, 1980.

Foegen, J. H. "Flexitime: The Way of the Future," *Administrative Management,* September 1980.

Friedman, Barry A. "Seniority Systems and the Law," *Personnel Journal,* July 1976.

Gannon, Martin J. "Four Days, Forty Hours: A Case Study," *California Management Review,* Winter 1974.

Gay, E. G. et al. *Manual for the Minnesota Importance Questionaire,* Minneapolis: Industrial Relations Center, University of Minnesota, 1971.

Gilbert, Geoffrey M. "Can Corporations Fund Employee Benefit Promises?" in David A. Weeks (ed.), *Rethinking Employee Benefit Assumptions,* New York: The Conference Board, Inc., 1978.

Glueck, William F. "Changing Hours of Work: A Review and Analysis of the Research," *The Personnel Administrator,* March 1979.

Goode, Robert V. "Complications at the Cafeteria Checkout Line," *Personnel,* November–December 1974.

Gordon, Josephine A. and Robert N. Schoeplein. "The Impact from Elimination of the Retirement Test," *Social Security Bulletin,* September 1979.

Gottschalk, Peter. "Employer-Initiated Job Terminations," Discussion Paper #589-79, Madison, Wisconsin: Institute for Research on Poverty, University of Wisconsin-Madison, 1980.

Goudy, Willis J. "Change in Retirement Plans: Findings from the Retirement History Study," draft, Washington D.C.: Office of Research and Statistics, Social Security Administration, 1979.

Green, Russell F. "Age, Intelligence and Learning," *Industrial Gerontology,* Fall 1973.

Grubbs, Michael Gene and Edward A. Powers. "A Multiple Measure Approach to the Relationship between Work and Retirement Attitudes," Miami, Florida: Department of Health and Rehabilitation, 1979.

Haberlandt, Karl F. "Learning, Memory and Age," *Industrial Gerontology,* Fall 1973.;

Hackman, J. R. and E. E. Lawler III. "Employee Reactions to Job Characteristics," *Journal of Applied Psychology,* 1971.

Harris, Louis. "1979 Study of American Attitudes Toward Pensions and Retirement," Conducted for Johnson and Higgins, February 1979.

Hedaa, Laurids. "Danish Survey Suggests Demotion for 'Obsolete' Managers: Finds Execs Prefer Lesser Jobs to Retirement," *World of Work Report Number 3*, 1980.

Henretta, John C. and Angela M. O'Rand. "Labor Force Participation of Older Married Women," *Social Security Bulletin*, August 1980.

Herzbert, F. B., R. O. Peterson, and D. F. Capwell. *Job Attitudes: Review of Research and Opinion*, Pittsburgh: Psychological Service of Pittsburgh, 1957.

Hewitt Associates. *Benefit Issues Regarding the Age Discrimination in Employment Act*, Compensation Exchange, Hewitt Associates, January 1980.

Hsiao, William C. "Raising the Retirement Age – Who Will Bear the Burden?" testimony presented to the U.S. House of Representatives Committee on Ways and Means, Subcommittee on Oversight, September 10, 1980.

Jacobson, Beverly. *Young Programs for Older Workers: Case Studies in Progressive Personnel Policies.* New York: Van Nostrand Reinhold Company, 1980.

Jaffe, A. J. and Jeanne Claire Ridley. "The Extent of Lifetime Employment of Women in the United States," *Industrial Gerontology*, Winter 1976.

Johnson and Higgins. *1979 Study of American Attitudes Toward Pensions and Retirement*, conducted by Harris Associates, New York: Johnson and Higgins, 1979.

Jones, Ethel B. and James E. Long. "Part-Week Work and Human Capital Investment by Married Women," *Journal of Human Resources*, Fall 1979.

Katzell, Raymond A. and Daniel Yankelovich. *Work, Productivity, and Job Satisfaction: An Evaluation of Policy-Related Research*, New York: Harcourt, Brace and Javanovich, Inc., 1975.

Keast, Fred D., Lois F. Copperman and Douglas G. Montgomery. "ADEA, Inflation, and the Retirement Decision," a paper prepared for the Gerontological Society, Washington D.C., November 1979.

_____ and Lois F. Copperman, "Determinants of Progressive Employment Policies for Older Workers," a paper prepared for the Gerontological Society, San Diego, November 1980.

Kenny, Martin. "Public Employee Attitudes Toward the Four-Day Week," *Public Personnel Management*, April 1974.

Koralik, Susan. "Implications of Government Policy-Making in Employee Compensation and Benefits," in David A. Weeks (ed.), *Rethinking Employee Benefits Assumptions*, New York: The Conference Board, 1978.

Krauss, Iseli K. "Cognitive Abilities in Older Workers," paper prepared for the Gerontological Society, Washington D.C., November 1979.

Kreps, Juanita M. *Lifetime Allocation of Work and Income.* Durham, N.C.: Duke University Press, 1971.

Lawler, Edward E., III. "New Approaches to Pay: Innovations that Work," *Personnel*, September–October 1956.

Linenberger, Patricia and K. Keaveny. "Age Discrimination in Employment: A Guide for Employers," *Personnel Administrator*, July 1979.

Litras, Thomas S. "The Battle Over Retirement Policies and Practices," *Personnel Journal,* February 1979.

Machaver, William V. "Employee Benefits: Promises and Realities," in David A. Weeks (ed.), *Rethinking Employee Benefits Assumptions,* New York: The Conference Board, Inc., 1978.

Mahoney, Thomas A., Jerry M. Newman and Peter J. Frost. "Workers' Perceptions of the Four-Day Week," *California Management Review,* Fall 1975.

Maklan, David M. *The Four-Day Workweek: Blue-Collar Adjustment to a Nonconventional Arrangement of Work and Leisure Time,* New York: Praeger Publishers, 1977.

Mamorsky, Jeffrey D. "Impact of the 1978 ADEA Amendments on Employee Benefit Plans," *Employee Relations Law Journal,* 1978.

Martin, N. H. and A. L. Strauss. "Patterns of Mobility within Industrial Organizations," in W. Lloyd Warner and N. H. Martin (eds.), *Industrial Man,* New York: Harper, 1959.

McCarthy, Maureen. "Trends in the Development of Alternative Work Patterns," *Personnel Administrator,* October 1979.

McConnel, Stephen R., Dorothy Fleisher, Carolyn E. Usher, and Barbara Hade Kaplan. *Alternative Work Options for Older Workers,* Los Angeles: The Ethel Percy Andrus Gerontology Center, University of Southern California, July 1980.

Maier, Elizabeth L. *Implications for Employment,* Washington D.C.: The National Council on Aging, 1976.

_____. *ERISA: Progress and Problems, An Early Assessment of the Pension Reform Law and Its Impact on Older Workers,* Washington D.C.: The National Council on Aging, 1977.

_____. "Pension Policy Goals: In A National Policy on Employment and Retirement," a paper prepared for the Gerontological Society, San Diego, November 1980.

_____ and Elizabeth Kerr. "Capabilities of Middle-aged and Older Workers: A Survey of the Literature," *Industrial Gerontology,* Summer 1976.

_____ and Cynthia Ditmar. *Varieties of Retirement Ages,* Staff Working Paper, Washington D.C.: President's Commission on Pension Policy, November 1979.

Meier, Elizabeth L. and Cynthia C. Dittmar. *Income of the Retired: Levels and Sources,* Washington D.C.: President's Commission on Pension Policy, October 1980.

Meyer, Mitchell and Harland Fox. *Profile of Employee Benefits,* New York: The Conference Board, Inc., 1974.

Morgan, James. Survey Findings presented at Conference on Work and Retirement, Andrus Gerontology Center, University of Southern California, February 1980.

Morrison, Malcom H. "The Future of Flexible Retirement," *College and University Personnel Association Journal,* Winter 1978.

Morse, Dean. *The Utilization of Older Workers,* a special report for the National Commission for Manpower Policy, Washington D.C.: National Commission for Manpower Policy, March 1979.

Mulanphy, James M. "Plans and Expectations for Retirement of TIAA-CREF Participants," paper prepared for the Gerontological Society, Washington D.C., November 1980.

Nealey, Stanley M. "Determining Worker Preferences Among Employee Benefit Programs," *Journal of Applied Psychology*, February 1964.

_____ and S. G. Goodale. "Worker Preferences Among Time-Off Benefits and Pay," *Journal of Applied Psychology*, August 1967.

Nollen, Stanley, Brenda B. Eddy, Virginia Martin and Douglas Monroe. *Permanent Part Time Employment: An Interpretive Review,* report prepared for the Employment and Training Administration, U.S. Department of Labor, Washington D.C., February 1976.

_____, Brenda B. Eddy, Virginia Martin. *Permanent Part Time Employment: The Manager's Perspective,* report prepared for the Employment and Training Administration, U.S. Department of Labor, Washington D.C., 1977.

_____. "Does Flexitime Improve Productivity?" *Harvard Business Review,* September–October 1979.

_____. *New Patterns of Work,* New York: Work in America Institute, Inc., 1979.

_____. "What is Happening to Flexitime, Flexitour, Gliding Time, the Variable Day? And Permanent Part-Time Employment? And the Four-Day Week?: The Changing Workplace," *Across the Board,* April 1980.

Rosen, Benson and Thomas H. Jerdee. "Too Old or Not Too Old," *Harvard Business Review,* November–December 1977.

Rosenbaum, James E. "Organizational Career Mobility: Promotion Chances in a Corporation during Periods of Growth and Contraction," *American Journal of Sociology,* July 1979.

Rosow, Jerome M. and Robert Zager. *The Future of Older Workers in America: New Options for an Extended Working Life,* Scarsdale, New York: Work in America Institute, Inc., 1980.

Rothman, Jack, John L. Erlich, and Joseph G. Teresa. *Promoting Innovation and Change in Organizations and Communities,* New York: John Wiley and Sons, 1976.

Schulz, James H. *The Economics of Aging,* Second Ed. Belmont, California: Wadsworth Publishing Company, 1976.

Shapiro, Kenneth P. "The Reversing Early Retirement Trend," *Personnel Administrator,* April 1980.

Sheppard, Harold L. and N. Q. Herrick. *Where have all the Robots Gone?* New York: Free Press, 1972.

_____ and Sarah E. Rix. *The Greying of Working America,* New York: Free Press, 1977.

_____ and Sarah E. Rix. "The Employment Environment and Older Worker Job Experiences," final report, Washington D.C.: American Institutes for Research, April 1979.

Sobel, Irwin. *Employment: Background and Issues,* 1971 White House Conference on Aging, Washington D.C. 1971.

Sonnenfeld, Jeffrey. "Dealing with the Aging Work Force," *Harvard Business Review,* November–December 1978.

Special Committee on Aging, United States Senate, Ninety-sixth Congress, 2nd Session. *Work after 65: Options for the 80's, Parts 1 and 2,*Washington D.C.: U.S. Government Printing Office, 1980.

———. *Emerging Options for Work and Retirement Policy,* Washington D.C., U.S. Government Printing Office, 1980.

Spencer, Charles D. and Associates, Inc. "ADEA Impact on Retirement Trends Seen as Minimal to Date," EBRI Research Reports, Chicago: Charles D. Spencer and Associates, 1979.

Stagner, Ross. "Propensity to Work: An Important Variable in Retiree Behavior," *Aging and Work,* Summer 1979.

Stewart, Gary M. and Arthur Guthrie. "Alternative Workweek Schedules: Which one Fits Your Operation?" *Supervisory Management,* June 1976.

Storey, James R. "Financial Disincentives for Continued Work by Older Americans," testimony before the House Ways and Means Subcommittee on Oversight, September 10, 1980.

Stromsdorfer, Ernst. *A Cost Benefit Analysis of Retraining,* unpublished Ph.D. Dissertation, St. Louis: Washington University, cited in Irwin Sobel, *Employment: Background and Issues,* Washington D.C.: 1971 White House Conference on Aging.

Swanson, Gordon I. and Jon Michaelson. *Manpower Research and Labor Economics,* Beverly Hills, California: Sage Publications, 1979.

Thumin, Fred J. "MMPI As a Function of Chronological Age," *Industrial Gerontology,* June 1969.

Towers, Perrin, Forster and Crosby (TFP&C). *Pensions, Social Security Benefits: Levels, Costs and Issues,* Washington D.C.: Business Roundtable, 1979.

Tracy, Martin B. "Flexible Retirement Features Abroad," *Social Security Bulletin,* May 1972.

U.S. News and World Report. "Battle of The Sexes: Men Fight Back," December 8, 1980.

Walker, James W. and Harriet L. Lazer. *The End of Mandatory Retirement: Implications for Management,* New York: John Wiley and Sons, Inc., 1978.

——— and Daniel E. Lupton. "Performance Appraisal Programs and Age Discrimination Law," *Aging and Work,* Spring 1978.

Wallfesh, Henry M. *The Effects of Extending the Mandatory Retirement Age,* New York: AMACOM, A Division of American Management Associations,1978.

Webster, Daniel. *Webster's Third New International Dictionary of the English Language, Unabridged,* Springfield, Massachusetts: G and C Merriam Company, Publishers, 1967.

Weeks, David A. (ed.). *Rethinking Employee Benefits Assumptions,* New York: The Conference Board, Inc., 1978.

Weitz, Harry. *The Foreign Experience with Income Maintenance for the Elderly,* Ottawa, Ontario: Minister of Supply and Services, 1979.

Werther, William B., Jr. "Mini-Shifts: An Alternative to Overtime," *Personnel Journal,* March 1976.

Yaffe, Rian M. "Changing Retirement Patterns: Their Effect on Employee Benefits," *The Personnel Administrator,* February 1979.

Index